THE LONGEST SUICIDE

THE LONGEST SUICIDE

The Life of a Manic-Depressive
Rare Book Dealer

David L. O'Neal

ARCHWAY
PUBLISHING

Archway Publishing books may be ordered through booksellers or by contacting:

Archway Publishing
1663 Liberty Drive
Bloomington, IN 47403
www.archwaypublishing.com
1 (888) 242-5904

ISBN: 978-1-4808-3112-4 (sc)
ISBN: 978-1-4808-3113-1 (e)

Library of Congress Control Number: 2016906980

Print information available on the last page.

Archway Publishing rev. date: 08/22/2016

Why I Write

I had always wanted to write and after 2002, when I retired from business, I had time to do so. I now write stories, essays and poems, and have had quite a few published in little magazines. When I was a child, I stuttered so badly that I sometimes couldn't talk at all. Even today, in late middle age, I am fearful of speaking under certain circumstances. (Parenthetically, I speak French too and have never stuttered in that language. I think this is because when speaking a foreign language well one assumes a different persona, new and freer, unencumbered by neurosis from the past. A mask to hide behind).

Consequently, I grew up apprehensive about verbal communication, distrusting speech as a mode of discourse for me. I was very uncomfortable with conversation and began to think oral communication led too easily to misunderstanding. So I learned, and prefer, to express myself in writing. Even in business, I tried to communicate with clients and colleagues in writing in order to make things clear and to give them time to consider and respond appropriately.

In addition, creative writing is good therapy. I am bipolar (bipolar II, mostly depressive) and have been hospitalized several times for my own protection when severely depressed. When mired in the swamp of depression, I regress into near infantilism and the old fear of becoming mute becomes nearly realized. While I cannot write during these times of extreme mental stress, at other times creative writing is very good therapy. Writing focuses the attention with laser-like precision and forces irrelevant thoughts out of the usual monkey-mind. In the heat of creating a poem, story, or essay—while processing ideas—it is impossible to dwell on much else. Thus, writing sweeps the mind of unpleasant thoughts and has healing power.

Writing is therapeutic and transformational in other ways too. It is therapeutic to write about specific personal issues or emotional problems, happy times as well as unhappy. A good deal of my poetry is written for this purpose, such as a poem on the distress of a recent divorce, love poems generated by unrequited desire, a poem on the agony of stuttering, a poem on the plight of the homeless, or an anti-war poem. Such writing doesn't solve the emotional dilemmas written about. Yet, in finally giving these issues full expression, their emotional impact can be pared down and more objectively understood. One can lighten one's baggage. Similarly, writing in anger about aggression takes the edge off. You write the mystery story instead of committing the murder!

It has been said that the core human condition is to be afraid of both life and of death and that our lives are experienced to be existential, serendipitous and chaotic. Another reason why I write is to impose some sort of order on these circumstances. Writing is a kind of control, a way to create order and shape meaning, to discover meaning in one's experience—even to discover wisdom. And to write creatively is sometimes to uncover deeply hidden emotions and ideas not ordinarily accessible to our consciousness. Still another reason to write is to capture, or recapture, memories or incidents worth recalling. It is like taking photographs, but the method is deeper, more reflective, and more analytical. Writing helps me to understand myself and my relation to other people and to nature. And writing poetry requires me to read a lot of poetry and critical works about poetry, as well as to understand the long poetic traditions of different languages. In this sense the writer's reading is educational and relaxing, like meditation.

Technically, my greatest pleasure as a writer is in revising:

fine-tuning, polishing, substituting an exactly right word or phrase for a merely nearly right one or for a wrong word—threshing out the chafe.

I am recently retired from the antiquarian book business during which career I wrote many catalogues offering rare books and manuscripts. I also wrote a number of professional articles about books, libraries and book collecting. Yet I always wanted to have time to write creatively, from the imagination. Now I have that time. Writing takes the time and fills it up—a good thing for someone subject to cycles of despair. Are not idle hands the Devil's playthings? Writing gives me purpose and lifts my consciousness from the triviality and mundanity of everyday life to a near transcendent mode. Creative writing lifts my mind to a mode of consciousness that perceives the expansiveness of the net of life as a whole. From lesser awareness to greater awareness.

While I write essentially for myself, getting one's work published is positive feedback. Without it you don't know if your stuff is any good. In the last analysis, I want people to read my writing. Further, getting published is an accomplishment, and accomplishment is one way for many of us to find meaning. There is aesthetic pleasure too: It is a pleasure to create beauty by putting the right words in the right order, a deeply felt enthusiasm when the writing is good and shows rhythm, pleasurable sound, and firmness of composition. And, yes, there is egoism too. There is, as George Orwell said, a "Desire to seem clever, to be talked about, to be remembered after death." Artists, writers, and composers all have to be a little mad to create in the first place, then even madder to let the work go forth and to assume someone else will enjoy it. Attempting to publish takes toughness and moxie.

But for me, the bottom line, the reason I write, is always the same: I cannot not write. I have the writing demon that keeps my soul uplifted from deep darkness. Writing is my shield against madness. Writing keeps me sane!

I was born in Miami, Florida, on March 17, 1938 which, being Saint Patrick's Day was a good day for an Irishman to be born. My parents were James and Eleanor O'Neal. My father had learned to fly in the Marine Corps. He was a tall (6 foot 3) good-looking man with blue eyes and brown hair. Some say he looked like the actor Jimmy Stewart. I mostly remember him dressed in his Pan Am uniform. He had a pronounced Georgia accent which he never lost.

D'Lo, Mississippi (cur. pop 400), previously Millhaven, once a thriving lumber-mill town, its name from old French maps: "De l'eau sans potable (water not drinkable),"thus De L'eau then D'Lo (my initials DLO) My father, James: born in D'Lo, 1908, raised in Gumbranch and in Macon, GA when attending Mercer University, came home in the Great Depression, sat rocking on the porch for two years in sweltering heat occasionally picking watermelons or other farm jobs; then got appointed, with help of congressman Carl Vinson, to the Army Air Corps where he flunked out, then Marine Corps Aviation where he learned to fly. He flew every plane from Boeing P-26 Peashooters to amphibious Clipper Ships, from 707s to 747s, high up in the wild blue above the earth for Pan American: first from Miami to Havana, then Miami to Caracas, Rio, other places in South America; New York to Europe, Africa, Russia; Los Angles to Tokyo, Hong Kong, Bangkok, Calcutta and beyond. He becoming Chief Pilot in New York, London, Berlin, and Frankfurt, refusing offers of administrative positions because he loved flying, loved it all his life. My Dad, from humble D'Lo, following his own *Declaration of Independence.*

My older sister, Barbara, was born to my mother in her first marriage. She was a pretty and talented woman. She had her hair in bangs, a wide mouth with a broad smile. Ed Curran later told me the principal of Roslyn High said that she attracted boys like flies. She was on the cover of *Vogue Magazine* with an article about her inside. She later went to Duke University on a full scholarship and became a stewardess for Pan American for a while. She was living in New York, came to see me several times at Princeton, and had gotten three standing room only tickets to *My Fair Lady* with the original cast of Rex Harrison and Julie Andrews. At the last minute she couldn't go so I came up to Manhattan from college with two roommates and we ended up getting front row center seats after standing for a few minutes. That was the first Broadway play I ever saw. Barbara was married twice. I used to go to Florida to see my parents, in Orlando, where they spent their last years, and also visited her. By that time, she had gotten Lupus and was an invalid.

My first memories are of our house in Miami, surrounded by other houses, on a level street (isn't Florida all flat!) with a small yard and a few trees and shrubs in the back which I remember playing in. When my father came home from work he dragged me to a cold shower with him. I yelled and cried. To this day I detest cold showers and I don't know why he did it. I never asked him!

Then I remember our homes in Coral Gables and Coconut Grove. In Coral Gables there was a large Banyan tree which I fell out of and broke my arm. And I saw a poisonous Coral snake in the window and hundreds of land crabs coming up the street when the tide was high. The crabs looked fierce to me. We then moved to Brownsville, Texas where I recall riding a horse with my father along the Rio Grande. I have some photographs of these days.

From Brownsville we went to Baltimore. I have seen the white steps in certain sections of Baltimore where we lived, but we weren't there long and I don't remember anything. Then we moved to Roslyn Estates, Long Island, New York. We lived in two houses there. Of the first I recall the painters on ladders outside drooling at my mother through the windows and I also recall the end of the war or hearing about it. From there we moved to another house, a nice place with four bedrooms and two baths. Our house was next that of Harder Wright, a lawyer in New York City who said he was always right and if we didn't believe him all we had to do was look at his mailbox. We got about five boys together and played football in Harder's back yard. He had beautiful flowers and we were a little afraid of Mr. Wright so we were careful not to mess his yard up. We then moved to another house which had four bedrooms and two baths, with a nice fireplace.

It was in this second house in Roslyn Estates. when I was about seven years old, that I met Ed Curran who became my best friend. We stayed there for about ten years. All during this time I stuttered very badly and blame the stuttering (in retrospect) on my father. Sometimes I could barely talk. He was a distant man and since he flew all over most of the world he had many good stories, but he never told them to me. My mother took me to a speech therapist in New York a few times, but it didn't work. My father would simply come home, have a few drinks, and read the newspaper. He rarely talked and hardly ever to me. Meal times were excruciating; it was usually dead silence.

Father You Left Before We Talked

Father, in silence you just walked;
It was your attention I sought.
Father, you left before we talked.

I chocked on words, sounds that fear balked.
Not hearing words for which I fought,
Father, in silence you just walked.

Father, with help I could have stalked
The words I'd have paid for, hard bought.
Father, you left before we talked.

I thought by you I might be mocked;
I raged, anguished, speechless, distraught.
Father, in silence you just walked.

I tried pain hard but painful gawked;
Stutter, stammer, the words caught.
Father, you left before we talked.

My tongue was to my palate caulked;
You could have brought the ease I sought.

Father, in silence, you just walked;
Father, you left before we talked.

My mother took me several times to the Saint Patrick's Day parade in New York City and said "this parade is for you, Dave." I think I believed it the first time. My father, by the way, was a good pilot but a poor businessman. He was one of the founders, with Al Ulchi, of Flight Safety which trained pilots by using simulators. Later Ulchi wanted the stock back and my father sold it to him. Flight Safety became worth billions and is now owned by Warren Buffet.

The Blizzard of '47

Some years ago our suburban lawn was extensive, and the unmowed grass was high, when my three and four-year-old niece and nephew visited us for the first time from New York City. When they got out of the car, their father had to carry them into our house because they refused to walk across the lawn. To these inner city kids, deprived of nature, the

*unfamiliar grass was like deep water or quicksand: they were
afraid to walk on it lest they sink in.*

About 2:00 o'clock in the afternoon on Thursday,
Christmas Day 1947, Ed Curran and I set out from Roslyn
Estates, Long Island, New York, to go camping. Ed and
I, eleven years old at the time, lived across the street from
each other and were best friends. With other friends, we
often played or camped in the dense woods of the MacKay
estate, which comprised 650 acres adjacent to the even larger
Whitney estate on Long Island's North Shore "Gold Coast."
We did other things in our own neighborhood such as ring
doorbells at night, play touch football on a neighbor's lawn or
stickball in a driveway, steal candy from Jackson's drugstore,
let air out of car tires, and drop sticks on passing cars from
trees overhanging the road between our homes. But camping
in the woods was special, especially during Christmas which,
being close to the promise of a New Year, was a foreword-
looking time and a time of regeneration.

It was cold. so Ed and I were dressed warmly in boots,
skull caps, wool scarves and winter jackets. Our knapsacks
held extra socks, sweaters, and mittens, as well as food, mess-
kits, tooth-brushes, toilet paper, a portable radio carried by
Ed that he had gotten for Christmas, matches, flashlights, and
extra water. Attached to the top of the knapsacks were our
sleeping bags and ponchos, and I had a folded entrenching
tool. From each of our radically shortened but still loose-
fitting army surplus web-belts dangled a canteen, a sheath-
knife, a small hatchet, a first-aid pouch, and a couple of MI
Carbine magazine pouches stuffed with candy we'd garnered
from our Christmas stockings. So we went clanking and
clattering south through Roslyn Heights to the Roselyn
Railroad Station where we picked up Rennie Witzig who

was similarly outfitted, if not quite so grandly. Jerry Chester, a classmate, and his older brother, Connie, were going to meet us at the campsite so we turned east at the Station and followed the tracks of the Long Island Railroad, which delineated the northern border of the forest, for about a mile and a half through MacKay country.

The Mackay estate had fallen into neglect after the Depression and its great house, Harbor Hill, had been torn down. Today the only reminders of the once-wooded MacKay Estate are two streets: Harbor Hill Road and MacKay Way. Most of the big estates in the area are gone now, suffering the same fate as the Mackay Estate: the woods cleared away and the land sold to developers for gated communities or more closely-packed housing developments. We boys played among the rubble ruins of house and in and around its overgrown gardens whose former glory was hinted at only by broken statuary, cracked and dried up fountains, low crumbling walls, and shrub-filled open space which formed overgrown clearings in the otherwise thick woods in which we delighted. Sometimes a bunch of us would go to these woods after school and play soldiers arrayed in squads against each other or some such war game because World War II was still much in our minds. At other times we would be Robin Hood and his Merry Men sword-fighting the minions of the evil Sheriff of Nottingham. Occasionally we would enact male rituals relating to our hormonal bodily changes at puberty.

As Ed and I and Rennie trudged along inside the tracks kicking up snow from the several inches that had fallen the Tuesday beforehand, the day was clear and crisp and nothing in the weather reports had indicated it would be otherwise. We talked about girls and about the Brooklyn Dodgers and about the several times we'd tried the dumb and dangerous game of lying down on one set of tracks while a train sped past on the other. And about how we'd chickened out each time by diving off into the bush beside the tracks. We also talked about the time Ed had gotten mixed up one late summer afternoon and went to our secret campsite expecting to rendezvous there with the rest of us. When no one showed up, he'd stayed by himself, ate, and slept on the ground until torrential rain woke him up about one o'clock in the morning. As he was putting on his poncho, Ed glimpsed, through the rain, underbrush, and trees, vehicle headlights approaching on an old, overgrown and barely navigable dirt road about a hundred yards away. Neither Ed nor any of us had ever seen anything moving on this abandoned road in the dense woods. When the truck stopped Ed snuck up to it in the down-pouring murk and saw the driver digging a hole. Frightened out of his wits, Ed had crept back to the campsite, gathered up his sodden stuff and high-tailed it for home.

In addition to being fun, the forest held magic and mystery and opened up deep places inside of us otherwise hidden, just as the expansive unconscious mind is often more fruitful than the shallower conscious mind. The forest, for us, was a place of adventure, of testing and initiation; a place of refuge and retreat away our elders; a place to get a glimpse of our own burgeoning adulthood; a place to leave behind the imaginary friends we'd lived with from books and daydreams and, instead, to grow and develop with real friends in a peer group. The forest was a place of some danger, real or imagined a place for transformation and fresh starts. Woods, with their ever growing trees, plants, bushes, and wild life, are places of abundant fertility where life thrives and luxuriates free from control. And this freedom to grow was exactly the developmental direction toward which we boys were tending. Maybe the deciduous great oaks, maples, elms, and birches which seasonally shed their leaves and grew new ones, were unconscious symbols to us of both strength and change, just as we might have taken the staunch year-round evergreens as symbols of immortality—perhaps reinforcing our own then youthful ideas that we'd live forever. The alluring woods, as I look back, were essential to our budding maturity and individuation. We were always glad to go into the forest; it is hard to imagine children growing up without nearby woods in which to romp. Today young persons are sent to wilderness camps to build character and self-sufficiency and adults go on nature quests seeking to find themselves. Not to have access to woods is to be deprived of one of the great benefits of nature. With all the past and current deforestation, what can it mean for children—for anyone—to no longer have access to woods? What can it mean to the human imagination not to possess such places? Surly we are all harmed and diminished when forests are diminished or destroyed?

Usually, for the camping, it was just Ed and I and Jerry, and one of Jerry's older twin brothers who were sixteen, Connie or Scott, from Roslyn Heights—all of us firmly middleclass—and sometimes other friends such as Rennie who lived literally on the other side of the railroad tracks near Roslyn High School. Connie had lost two fingers of his left hand fooling around with nitroglycerine in the Chester's basement. The formidable Chester twins were tough and smart. Both had throwing knives and .22 rifles for target practice and were legendary in Roslyn for their sangfroid and martial arts skills. Among other threatening moves and holds, it was rumored that their bear-hugs could suffocate a person. Connie and Scott did physics and chemistry experiments at home and competed academically so that when one was usually at the head of their class, the other was right behind. They were good role models for us, unusual and cool take charge guys whom we held in awe.

In addition to taking us camping, the Chester twins also led us on long hikes through places we were not supposed to be, such as the gravel pits north of Roslyn (which meant that we had to pass through a junkyard with an old man and his scary dog), the Roslyn wetlands, some dry-caked mud flats, and the dusty grounds of the nearby cement plant. On these surreptitious expeditions, over flat ground, embankments, and hills, we were, in our minds, Army Rangers in enemy territory, covert OSS agents, or, sometimes, stealthy Indians traversing hostile pale-face settlements.

When had gone far enough following the railroad tracks, we came to the turn-off we'd marked with a couple of ropes tied to a tree, and headed south through the mostly leafless deciduous winter forest in the direction of the campsite which was about a half-mile further on. Off to the right, about a hundred yards from the indistinct path but not visible from it, was a frozen over pond. We heard Jerry and Connie's voices coming from the direction of the pond so we headed over to them and found that the brothers, using fresh cut pine boughs as brooms, had swept off a portion of the pond and were playing hockey, without skates, with branches as hockey sticks and a pine-cone as the puck. We shed out gear and played with them for about 45 minutes, slipping and sliding all the while, ganging up on Connie when he had the puck, laughing, and spending more time prone on the ice than moving erect above it. Then we went to the campsite.

We had discovered the campsite two years before; it was natural, simple, comfortable and, above all ours—hidden to those not in our clique and from other prying eyes—included those of parents. The site was in a copse of long-needled evergreen pines and hemlocks. There was light groundcover but very few shrubs in the copse and the trees were old enough so their lowest branches were over our heads and we could easily walk upright among them. One of the trees had sheltering branches so perfectly circular and so full with thick needles that it was an ideal sanctuary—even from rain. Deep within the surrounding forest of oak, maple, birch and elm trees, our stand of evergreen pines was a sacred grove unto itself; our campsite was contained within the woods but somehow separate from it. Near the tracks, one hot summer day, we had come across a pile of railroad ties carefully stacked for future replacement by railroad workers. We had hauled the railroad ties laboriously to the campsite and out of this cache we made a semi-circular bench, the seat being four ties wide, the backrest four ties high. The main support behind the bench was the tree trunk itself augmented on the wings by posts behind it as well as piled up rocks and dirt. About six feet from the middle of the length of the bench, we'd dug a fire-pit for warmth and cooking and lined it with rocks. Scott had supplied an old grate which we could lay on the rocks across the fire for cooking meat. We'd also dug a latrine behind some thick bushes about forty yards away. Wood was plentiful: there were a lot of dead, dry branches lying about that we could break into smallish pieces of kindling as well as larger pieces we could cut up with our hatchets, leaving the really big pieces for Connie to split. Connie had taught us how to start a friction fire by rubbing two sticks together, but the method was a lot of work and far from foolproof; when the sun was strong we often started our fires with dry grass ignited by a magnifying glass; usually we brought paper to help get the fire started or as back up if the other methods failed. Before we left the forest, we always tried to leave some good wood stacked up for our next visit.

In summer we brought pup tents and dug drainage ditches around the outside of the tents to direct rain water away from us. There was nothing worse than waking up soaking wet from water in a tent. But camping in winter was special: there were no mosquitoes, bugs or gnats, there was no rain or mud, and everything was clean and crisp. Aside from the cold which, being warm-blooded boys, we could handle okay, camping in the winter was fun. There was a clean purity to it.

The first thing we did when we got to the campsite that Christmas Day was take our gear off and pool our food. We gave the food to Connie who put it all in a duffle bag he'd brought for that purpose. Then we hung the food bag and packs on some low lying branches. We brushed off what little snow was on the seat then gathered kindling and firewood and made a fire. It was beginning to get gray and we knew it would be dark soon. We had a good, warming meal of grilled hamburgers, and corn and baked potatoes wrapped in tinfoil and placed directly in the fire. We also had hot chocolate and, for dessert, roasted marshmallows. Then we threw snow on the fire to put it out. When there were only a few glowing coals, we set out in the dark to go to the movies in Roslyn Village.

Ed and I often went to Saturday morning matinees which cost 25 cents; then, if we hadn't stuffed ourselves with popcorn and candy, we'd have a hamburger and coke afterward for another 25 cents. I remember the old westerns. And I especially remember those scary shorts where a villain tied a pretty woman to a conveyor belt that was moving toward a circular saw … "to be continued next week" Would she escape a horrible fate? These Saturday movies were usually double-features and when we came out we'd be nearly blinded by the daylight. But going to the movies at night was special and we only did it when camping. Getting to the Village in the dark from our campsite wasn't easy. There was no visible trail from our campsite that night so Connie had to take us there by compass course most of the way. We made sure we all had flashlights, stayed close together, and walked in our leader's footsteps. We had to go northeast, back over the tracks then mostly downhill, in single file through heavy brush to the Village. It took about 30 minutes going down to the village and 45 minutes back up. Because none of us wanted to be last, we drew straws for that position. Needless to say some fearful predator-like animal noises were made by one or the other of us, but for the most part trips to the movies and back at night were made in silence.

When we got back to the woods we built up the fire again and sat around it for a while, talking about the movie and about Christmas, whittling wooden whistles and other things with our knives, and watching the snow come down in the copse. The flickering fire-flames and the light from a kerosene lantern that Connie had brought cast marvelous shadows among the trees and other foliage, onto the ground-snow and around and onto ourselves. We smelled of wood-smoke and happiness. Then we put our ponchos down for ground cover, spread our mummy-shaped down-filled sleeping bags over the ponchos, and pulled the openings tight over our heads. It had been a good day and we were tired. So we slept and dreamt.

The woods were a dream world to us, a place populated by strange dream-induced creatures, a place where our unconscious minds could surface and our imaginations could reign. Throughout history and literature outlaws and outcast, the bewildered and the ecstatic, fairy tale characters and adolescents have all sought asylum and protective shelter in woods. While our suburban homes were the center of our normal, ordinary lives and were the places we came back to, we went, temporarily, to the woods and in coming back out of them were always changed a little. Without the opportunity to experience the exteriority of forests, without such outsides, there are no contrasting insides. Those who dwell only within the cleared space of city or suburb, within only the space of institutionalized order, are deprived and disadvantaged. What happens to the wonder and poetry of life when the forests are gone? And so we slept and dreamt on as our deepest often buried selves unfolded in the woods.

I awoke first in the morning, about 8:00 o'clock. Initially it was dark because I was completely covered with seven or eight inches of snow. When I sat up and shook off the covering snow it was still gray because snow was falling so rapidly that it obscured the light of day. Ed, Rennie, Jerry, and Connie were just lumps in a field of white snow, like small Indian mounds in winter. After a short time, at different intervals, their heads would pop up and they'd get up, shake like dogs shedding water, and join me at the fire I had made. We learned later that it had started to snow about 3:00 AM. It was quiet and peaceful, beautiful and enchanting. Snow fell silently as we had breakfast; it fell through the pine trees in the copse where, every so often, a branch would shake loose or bend to the point of dumping its burden of accumulated snow. But under our special sheltering tree, with its warming fire, we experienced little of the fullness of the growing blizzard. We boiled eggs hard in the pans of our mess-kits, fried bacon, used tinfoil to make biscuits from the ubiquitous Bisquick, and brewed hot tea. After breakfast we rolled snowballs and made them into a magnificent snowman. And, there were the obligatory snowball fights, of course, most of which pitted the Chester brothers against Ed, and Rennie and I. We also practiced throwing our knives in such a way that they would stick and quiver into trees. The knives had to be thrown carefully because if you missed a tree the knife would likely disappear into the snow beyond, to be found only with difficulty. Our knives failed to stick more often than not, although Connie was good at it. Then we cleaned our pots and pans with snow, put them and other equipment in our packs, then dug out our sleeping bags and ponchos and secured them on top of our packs. It was so pleasant in the woods in the blizzard that we decided to linger and stayed for lunch: chicken-noodle soup this time, with more Bisquick biscuits, chocolate chip cookies for desert. Then we left.

By the time we started home about two feet of snow had accumulated, which we discovered once we left the copse because out of the shelter of the tall pines the ground was covered with thick heavy snow. There was wind, but not the freezing, howling wind of a typical blustery blizzard. This storm came from the southeast rather than the west or northwest from which such blizzards usually come on the east coast. It was a heavy snowfall and damp: the storm had gathered moisture and momentum over the Gulf Stream. When we exited the woods and went west along the railroad tracks, we experienced, more or less, a whiteout: everything, including the woods on both sides of us, disappeared; everything was hidden and confused and earth and sky seemed bound together in a limitless and spiritual manner. The snow was accumulating rapidly and it was hard going. As we shuffled along and stayed close together, just as we had coming and going to the movies the evening before, Connie lead the way intentionally shortening his stride to accommodate our smaller strides and we stepped in his footprints. It was so quiet we could hear ourselves breathing and such tough going that we were pretty soon perspiring. But we were after all, in our minds, now an advanced patrol of the 10th Mountain Division in Nazi occupied Norway, well used to fighting in harsh terrain and severe weather. When we got back to the railroad station, we parted company with the Chesters and with Rennie. Then we plodded straight north up the middle of Warner Avenue that led directly to Mineola Avenue across which was our street, Intervale, which led up and into Roslyn Estates and to our homes. There was not a single car on Warner Ave, nor a snowplow; it seemed like the whole world had gone inside their homes and that Heaven and the Earth were fused by a pearly infinity of falling snow. We couldn't see the Christmas wreaths on doorways because of the poor visibility, but lighted Christmas trees glowed a pale, eerie yellow from snow-specked windows. Except for an occasional hushed whoosh muffled by the snow when a clump of it slid off a rooftop, there was very little sound. Cars on the street were beginning to look like polar bears, the snowflakes were like a multitude of white sky-whirling feathers, and the snow seemed to be falling from the beginning of time. When we crossed Mineola Avenue with its little clutch of stores and shops, the few people we saw looked like ghosts while nearby surrounding objects disappeared.

Ed and I, by this time covered in white, parted company in the middle of our street and I wallowed up my long unplowed driveway. Mother answered the back door and greeted me with relief. She asked if I had seen my father because he and Cliff Curran, Ed's father, fearful we were in trouble because of the blizzard, had gone out to find us at about 9:00 that morning and hadn't come back. Of course we'd never told our parents exactly where the campsite was so there was no chance they would find it in a blizzard somewhere in a couple of square miles of forest. And so, after four hours of stumbling around in rapidly accumulating snow with steadily deteriorating visibility, our fathers gave up and returned home cold and exhausted. I had already gone for a nap; when I woke up an hour and a half later, my father was dozing by a fire in the living room. Mother later told me that when he rang the front doorbell she told him to "go around to the back door" so as not to track snow into the front rooms; my father gave her a hard look and came in by the front.

How disappointed we would have been had our fathers found us and told us to go home—like wayward little boys! It would have been tantamount to punishment. One of the purposes of camping out was to be on our own, not to be found, to be away from adults. If our fathers had found us, our sense of accomplishment at managing very well indeed in a blizzard, our sense of independence, would have been greatly diminished—*we* would have been diminished. To be found, to be "found out," and "rescued" by our fathers would have broken a magical spell we'd weaved around ourselves. In the blizzard of '47, the worst since 1888, we'd outdone our fathers.

It eventually snowed for almost 24 hours and accumulated nearly 27 inches. When we awoke in the morning the following day, the sun shone on a wondrous Antarctic-like environment with drifts here and there up to 10 feet. Snow blanketed windows and doors, cars were snowed under on the streets and stuck for days, snowplows heaped mountains of snow into parking lots and formed giant sidewalls to slippery streets, buses didn't run, and you could safely jump out of second story windows. For weeks we built snow forts and igloos and dug tunnels and went sledding and skiing and sliding on the nearby hills of Plandome Golf Course. During this time Ed and I and our friends truly had the minds of winter: we beheld with joy frost on the boughs of pine trees crusted with snow and the spruces were rough in the glitter. Those were the days we flourished like the evergreens in the snowy copse of our campsite. Those were the days in which we grew and lived.

Ed Curran

Eddo Curran and I
lived across the street from each other in grammar school
in Roslyn, Long Island, New York.
We were best friends.

Being red-blooded boys
grown out of our Tinker Toys,
we did risky stuff.
We rang doorbells at night
then hid behind trees while our victims shouted
"You boys are sleaze!"
We dropped sticks on passing cars
from branches hanging over Leafy Way;
we let air out of car tires and poured sand in car's gas tanks;
we rang fire alarms.
We did unspeakable things.
Ed was a year younger
so was obliged to pick on him sometimes.
I threw ice-balls at him that were hard and dense
or made Ed's sled crash into the fence.
I threw rocks into a fort of leaves
Ed was hiding behind
and he needed stitches in his left ear.
Once I threw a dart at him
which briefly stuck
in the back
of Ed's
head
before
fall-
ing
out.

One day Ed butted me in the nose.
His head was hard, it hurt.
I never bullied him again.
Then I moved far away.

Ed Curran and I met again after fifty years.
We live in the same city,
sail on his boat,
and drink to each other's health.
Sometimes I want to look
for scar tissue behind Eddo's ear
and on the back of his head.
But I never will
because we're best friends
And that's where it ends.

In Roslyn I had a Golden Retriever named Coffee because of his color. My father didn't want a dog in the house at night, so Coffee went across the street and slept with Ed Curran who had a room in the basement. But one evening, when my parents were out, Coffee and I were in the downstairs study listening to the Green Hornet on the radio when the hair stood straight up on Coffee's back, then he ran to the back door and the door slammed shut. It was dark outside and coffee had probably chased off a burglar. On another occasion Coffee was sitting next to my brother who mistakenly (I think, more later) sat on his tail. Coffee bit my brother's friend instead. After all, you can't bite the family. Eventually Coffee bit a neighbor's little girl and had to be put away.

My mother, born in 1909, was a direct descendant of English pilgrims who settled in American in the 1600's. Paternally she was of

the Everett family which came over on the Mayflower in 1620. She
was a pretty woman, energetic and with a nice smile.

I got nervous going into my parent's
mysterious bedroom
that was connected to mine by a shared bathroom.
When my mother exercised with no clothes on
I went into the bathroom and peeked through the keyhole.
She did her exercises undressed
in front of windows that faced the street.
When she touched her toes and moved her arms around
her breasts jiggled up and down
and her nipples stuck out like cherries,
her long brown hair swung from side to side,
and her neck arched like a swan's.
I saw brown hair between her legs,
And her bottom and shoulders were curvy.
Her skin was smooth and white like pearls.
She was so pretty, and so naked;
I couldn't keep my eyes off her.
I looked and looked,
trying not to breath loud, not to cough,
trying to be quiet as in church.
But I could tell she knew I was watching.
Maybe neighbors were watching too.
Maybe that's what she wanted.

She kept exercising every day
after I came home from school.
And I kept watching.
It was our secret.
And I kept watching.

A Child's Winter

The whitest snowflakes,
like a multitude of little stars loosened from the heavens,
settle on the blue spruces encircling the sloping
lawn of our New England house on the hill.
A single streetlight glows nearby,
and the evergreens glitter in the gloaming.
I am sledding on my flexible-flyer
into the spruces which shield me from the slippery road.
When I slide into the trees, snow
shakes loose from their branches and shivers down my neck.
My dog, a golden retriever, enjoys this winter game
and bounds through the snow beside me.
Under wet gloves and socks, my hands and feet are cold.
As the day darkens, Mother beckons from the doorway;
it is time to go in.
I smell the comforting scent of fresh laundry
in the pantry and trudge up the slope
through the deepening snow while the dog prances ahead.
I will get a warm bath, then a good supper
and mother will read *The Song of Hiawatha* to me
before a crackling fire in the living room.

Accident

One summer, when I was about ten years old, my father invited to
our farm in Pennsylvania, my southern grandmother and grandfather,
and my four cousins Libba, Billy, Ellen and Ben. Ben was the oldest
and was about fourteen.

Dad had planted a patch of sweetcorn among the corn we fed
the animals and when it ripened we all shucked corn. We also picked
raspberries. blue berries and other stuff, raced sticks (as boats) in the
creek, and generally had a fine time. Ben was a good worker who
liked to work around the farm. One-day Ben, who was tall, had sandy
hair and a square jaw, was using the threshing machine about three-
quarters of a mile from the house. He was greasing the strap which
ran the flywheel when his had slipped. Ben screamed, looked at the
torn tendons in his left wrist, and told me to drive the tractor home.
I had never driven a tractor before but off we went both crying all the
while. We got to the farm house and Ben was taken to the hospital.
It ended his basketball career.

The Gun

To this day I don't know exactly why I pointed that loaded gun
at my father. We had been hunting in the late afternoon on the farm
he had in Pennsylvania near the Delaware Water Gap. My father
was a gentleman farmer: we still lived in Roslyn and a tenant farmer,
Clive, ran the farm. My father sent my mother and me to the farm
for a month or so in the summers. He joined us there when he could.
I say he *sent* us because Mother and I didn't like the farm much. My
mother didn't like being away from her middle-aged friends, bridge
partners, and parties. And I hated being away from my friends who
I knew were living it up back home: swimming, playing stick-ball,
riding bikes, going to matinee movies together, throwing sticks at cars
at night. Once, when told we were going to the farm, I ran away and
hid in a half-built house next door to ours.

Clive and his wife had two daughters, somewhat younger than
me, and I played with them a little when we first got the farm. I
used to wrestle with them until Clive thought it was dangerous or
something and told his girls they couldn't wrestle with me anymore.

He was probably a little right because I was beginning to like to shimmy up trees in the woods and rub my private part against the rough bark.

My father, as I've said, was a pilot for Pan American who was away for long periods of time. That he was away so much was all the more reason to want his attention when he was home. But I didn't get it. I suppose he and I got along well enough, except he seldom talked to me. Tall, taciturn, and intimidating, my father was not a big talker and rarely showed emotion. He'd come home from work, have a couple of whiskies, and then read the newspapers. Dinner times were excruciating: the silence was deafening. I developed an embarrassing stutter. The stutter got worse when I tried to address him, to the point where I could hardly talk when he was around. Since it took me forever to say something, he'd get impatient and turn away. Which made matters worse. This tense dynamic was a real self-reinforcing bummer. I'd get frustrated, then angry at him, then angry at myself, then depressed because I didn't express my anger directly. I didn't ask questions at school because I was afraid I'd stutter and be mocked. Which I did and was, often. The stuttering, mostly because of my father, caused me great mental pain. And of course my father was an authority figure. For years I had trouble addressing authority figures such as bankers and lawyers, or anyone who was tall, brooding, and foreboding.

On the farm, I hunted for squirrel by myself with the .22 rifle my father bought me. Squirrels were hard to get. They were a small target, much smaller, for instance, than my father's head, even when he was at a distance. If a squirrel saw you coming it would scurry around to the other side of the tree trunk. You had to hit a squirrel with the first shot, usually when it was way up in the branches, because the squirrel would take off like a rocket after the crack of a bullet. But when I got one, my mother would skin and cook it Squirrels taste like chicken. We had a pond at the farm which was full of frogs, and I used to shoot them too. Frogs explode into a mess. There was also a stream in the woods with small fish in it. I shot them too. But a .22 won't penetrate water very far; once in a while a fish would float to the top, concussed, and be swept away downstream.

Other than shoot, there was almost nothing to do at the farm. We didn't have a television, there was no nearby town with movies, and I had no friends there whatsoever. So I read a lot. I liked murder mysteries and horror stories, especially. I could help Clive bring in hay and do other stuff with him, but I wasn't big on being a farm hand. In fact, I wasn't big on work of any kind. I liked to watch people work, including seeing Clive slaughter the hogs. Clive would shoot the hogs in the ear first, and then cut their throats.

Our house in Roslyn was heated with coal which was sucked into the furnace down a hole in the coal bin. My job was to get in the bin and shovel coal over the hole when necessary. I'd come out black—nose, eyes and ears choked with coal dust—and I resented that dirty job. At school I learned that if you said "My father works in a shipyard" holding your tongue on the last word it comes out "shityard". I did this within earshot of my father when he was in the bathroom. He really got mad. The next day I stole some money from his dresser. One time, when I was watching, my father was ice-skating on our neighborhood pond and fell in where the ice was thin in the middle. I suppose everybody has wished someone dead at one time or another: a cheating spouse, a distant and seemingly uncaring parent, a friend who turns on you. But of course, for most people, these are fantasies.

Groundhogs make a mess of farmers' fields because they heap a lot of dirt up when digging out their holes and underground tunnels. Their mounds can dull or break the blades of mowing machines. So I hunted groundhogs, which were easier targets than squirrels. You had to get downwind of the hole, then lie or sit quietly until a groundhog popped up to eat, which was usually in the late afternoon. Groundhogs don't see so well but they have a keen sense of smell. Sometimes I could see one wiggling its nose, sniffing the air, leery.

Once you shot at one, hit or miss, it would be a long time before others would come out of the ground.

I was lying in a field waiting for a groundhog to pop up one day when a red fox just sauntered past me not too far away. I killed the fox with one shot, brought it to the farmhouse, put it on the porch, and ran excitedly up to the bedroom where my mother and father were having a nap. My father didn't believe I had gotten a fox, though I swore it. He only believed me after seeing the evidence. I was never quite sure my father believed much of anything I painfully said.

The sins of my father toward me were those of omission and lack of attention: He never praised me or told me I could do something or that I was able or good; he never encouraged me or said I could be whatever I wanted to be, even though I was a good student and not bad at sports either. And he rarely engaged me directly. What little I got about what he was thinking or feeling came from my mother: "Your father thinks you should go to bed at nine; your father says for you to cut the grass." And so forth. About the time I was twelve, I had begun to feel my father didn't think well of me, that maybe he really didn't like me much. I didn't know what to do to get his approval. This neglect didn't visibly piss me off so much as make me sad, bitter.

Anyway, my father and I were hunting groundhogs that afternoon, me with a .22 and he with the shotgun. We were propped up against two bales of hay in the corner of a field downwind from where we expected the little beasts to come out. But none did. It was getting dark, clouding up and threatening rain. We were about to leave when I saw a rabbit moving around in a hedgerow about fifty yards away. I aimed, took a deep breath, fired, and hit the rabbit squarely. When I reached it, the rabbit was shuddering from shock and one of its eyes was shot out. As I watched that poor defenseless, bloodstained and once cuddly creature die, I felt such great shame and disgust with myself. After that I never shot another animal.

When I turned to go, my father was already on the dirt road to home, about as far away as the rabbit had been. I reloaded the gun by habit. Just as I took a bead on my father's head, he turned around and saw me aiming at him. And flinched. What was I thinking when I had my father in my sights? Just thoughtlessly aiming at someone, as boys will do? Was I horribly disappointed in him and boiling over with years of pent up frustration? Was I enraged that he had just walked away without talking, as he had so often done in the past. Was I temporarily insane? Did I really mean to kill him?

I was grateful to Dad for teaching me how to shoot straight. He died peacefully at eighty-five a few years ago.

When I was about eleven, there was a bully who lived on the wrong side of the tracks in Roslyn who used to terrorize me some days when I was walking home alone from school. So I decided to have Edith walk with me to protect me. Edith was a black girl, a tough cookie, also from the other side of the tracks, who could really flail her arms and fight. It worked. Charlie was another friend but not bright. On day Charlie came to our house and put his report card on the kitchen table. My mother saw the report card and thought it was mine. It gave her quite a start until I explain why there were mostly Ds and some failures. We gave a Halloween party in the dark attic of our home. There were about twelve kids including Edith. My father played the part of the ghost and was dressed in a sheet. When he jumped out of a closet Edith screamed and screamed. Then, for some reason Walter, another friend, hit me hard in the stomach during recess at school. Later, Walter and went to a circus in Roslyn Village and when confronted by two toughs, he put his hand in his pocket as if he had a knife. That did it and they walked off.

I continued to stutter miserably.

Georgia On My Vine

I swear to God I've never been so scared in my life. I swear it. What saved me, sure as hell, were the prayers our grandmother made us all say before bed, before she put her dentures in the water glass on the edge of the bathroom sink. You know, like **"Now I lay me down to sleep, I pray the Lord my soul to keep."** And the Lord's Prayer too, I mean especially the part that goes **"deliver us from evil."**

When we were youngsters our parents packed us off to Macon, Georgia, for several summers to stay with our grandparents at their home on the southern edge of town. Ben and Ellen Anne, my cousins from Columbia, South Carolina, were fifteen and ten and were brother and sister. Billy and his sister Mary Lou were eight and ten and came down from Atlanta. For me, eleven, it was an exotic adventure because I was from Massachusetts. Macon, with its red clay, strange vegetation, and stifling heat was different, and my grandparents and first cousins talked slow and different too. They said things like "fetch," "y'all," "aksed" and "over yonder." When our grandfather, Paps, got out of sorts, which he rarely did because he taught Sunday School, Grandmother (Minnie Pearl, I learned later) said he was "tearing up the pea patch;" and when it was time she'd say to us "go on wash up because we're fixin' to eat supper in ten minutes." Ellen Anne, blond curls with blue-eyes and always happy, was cute as pie and I took a shine to her. But nothing ever happened because you can't smooch with a cousin. Billy was fat, had blond bangs, and looked funny in his shorts which bunched up around his crack. Ben once told me, secretly, that Billy was "three bricks short of a load." Mary Lou was chubby too. She had green eyes and black hair and a down-turned mouth. I thought she was spoiled and stuck-up, and she picked on Billy a lot. I was glad I wasn't him. Being the oldest, and by far the biggest, Ben was our leader. He had short brown hair and a handsome, suntanned face, played basketball in high school and was pretty smart, I thought. He took us to the Maxie Gregg

public swimming pool, about a mile away, and made the biggest belly
floppers of anyone. And Ben would lead us ("ankling down the hill,"
he said) to the little zoo in Memorial Park. The zoo had different kinds
of birds and small animals but, thank God, no snakes.

The summer before the one I'm talking about, Eddie Leary, the
bully who lived across the street, stuffed Ben into the sewer pipe beside
the road. But the pipe was dry and Ben didn't cry. By this summer
Ben had grown in so much of a spurt that he and Eddie had a sort
of standoff. Ben protected us against Leary or at least got us into the
house and locked the doors so that all the bully could do was look in
the windows and make scary faces. And when we played Kick the Can
in the street with some friends while the bats (who could get in your
hair, Ben said) fluttered around the streetlights in the twilight, Ben
could kick the can twice as far as anybody. So I looked up to Ben and
believed most everything he said. Although one time he persuaded
me to eat some elephant ears which he said tasted good and sweet.
I did eat some and threw up they were so bitter. Grandmother took
Ben by his own ear and pulled him into the house. We could hear
her shouting, and Ben never did much like that again. It was odd but
Ben never cussed. Maybe because Paps was a Sunday school teacher,
but I don't think Ben cussed at home in Columbia either. He'd say
"dad gumit" or "goll digit" or "oh shucks"—nothing' worse. Not even
"frig it."

If it was raining or if we had nothing better to do, we'd swing
in the heat on the porch on the long wooden swing-seat that four of
us could get into, and try to touch the railing with our bare feet. Or
play Chinese checkers with Paps. Our grandfather had failed a couple
of times in the lumber business and, somewhat to grandmother's
disdain, was a clerk in a grocery store. At night we'd often catch
fireflies and put them in jars. We punched holes in the jar tops so
the fireflies could breathe and wouldn't die. Sometimes we played
"sardines;" when all but one of us were bunched up hiding together
behind a hedge or bush we couldn't keep from laughing. The woods

were one of our favorite places when we were feeling adventurous. It was thick with huge longleaf pines, slack pines, ferns, cattails, thorn bushes, white oaks, poplars, and loblolly. In most of the woods the ground was soft and mulched over with pine needles and rotting leaves, as well as fallen branches and decaying logs. Some of the big pine trees were surrounded by thickets of bushes and vines which, if you could get through them, made neat hiding places because there were a couple of feet of space between the thickets and the tree trunks and you were invisible there. Also there were vines to swing on, vines all over the place, many of which would hold your weight.

When we went into the woods we always went single file down the path, like Ben told us to do. But there was a hitch. Ben said that the first person in line woke the snake up, the second person maybe stepped on it or frightened it, and the third person in line got bit by a mean, pissed off snake. There were real bad snakes in those woods too—there really were! As you'll see. I mean rattlesnakes, copperheads, coral snakes and cottonmouth water moccasins. I only ever saw the water moccasin, never any of the others. And I suppose Ben was putting us on to some extent and that there weren't really that many snakes. But I know I heard a rattler once, and I could swear I heard the others swishing around in the underbrush. I had nightmares about snakes. Snakes will eat rats, you know, and we had some rats under the house. So snakes were probably under there too, which is why none of us ever crawled under the house. And I'm pretty sure that snakes liked to eat the overripe figs which fell on the ground beside the fig tree in the yard, and maybe they'd slither up the pomegranate bush too. That's why I was careful around those fruits.

Anyway, when we went into the woods, nobody wanted to be third in line so there was always a lot of jittin' about, jockeying for position in the line, trying not to be third. Billy was third a lot and we all thought Billy was lucky not to ever get bit. I always went into the woods with my high-top sneakers and three pairs of knee-length white socks which I had bought, before going to Georgia that summer, expressly for snake protection purposes. Ben always carried a hatchet in the woods stuck into his belt, as well as a knife. He got real good at throwing the hatchet so that it stuck in trees. In fact he used to practice a lot throwing the hatchet at trees in the yard until Grandmother stopped him from doing that because it was bad for the trees: they ended up with slit marks in them which sometimes oozed sap. Ben told us he carried the knife so he could make an emergency cut and suck the poison out if any of us got snake-bit!

The path we had tramped down into the woods went for about a half-mile and led to a wide part of the creek where the water pooled and ran slow and was about two feet deep. At the beginning of a summer we (mostly Ben with his hatchet) had cleared away brush and stuff on both sides of the wide place in the creek because there was a great swinging vine at that spot hanging off a stout limb of a large oak. The vine was three-quarters of an inch thick where you gripped it and was the most perfect swinging vine you'd ever want to see. You got on a big fallen log, about a foot off the ground, swung over the creek, and landed on another log on the far side. That is, you landed right if you got sufficient momentum on the swing to get to the other side. If not, and you ended up short of the far-side log, you couldn't quite get back to where you started. Then you'd dangle over the creek until either one of the cousins helped you, or you fell in, or you maneuvered enough to step down onto one of the exposed flattish rocks in the creek. The water was cold but, since most days were hot, falling in was okay, even fun. If it were really sweltering, we'd let go and drop into the cooling water on purpose. Billy fell in the most and often went home to grandmother soaking wet, sometimes crying. Ben never once fell in. The girls and I fell in a few times.

Now I was thin so, not weighing much, I was a good vine-swinger and could hold my weight pretty good. So when we got to the creek that day, I swung on the vine first. But my foot slipped so I didn't get a good swing. Not enough, anyway, to get to the other side. So I dangled over the creek, swinging slowly and looking down for a good rock. I saw a pretty good rock close to where I hung and was about to let go and step off on it when I saw a large dark greenish-black snake curled up on the top of the rock getting some sun where the canopy of the woods was thin. The snake was slowly moving its head back and forth in a short arc and was the scariest looking thing I ever saw. Its mouth was half open and I could see its evil fangs. Ben, who was standing at the side of the creek, saw the snake too, about the same time, and frantically whispered to me "Hush, hush, Cottonmouth. Be still." Billy and the girls were ranged close around the area and had been talking and laughing, but they suddenly shut up and stood stark still too.

The Cottonmouth water moccasin is about the deadliest snake in all of Georgia—in all of North America, as a matter of fact. I knew that and was positioned two feet above it and slightly to the right. The vine was still swaying a bit and the bottom end of it was only a few inches above the snake. Sometimes, when stuck in the middle, you could get the vine swinging again by moving your body back and forth just right. But Ben motioned to me to hang still because, I guess, he didn't want me to call more attention to myself and irritate the snake, although the ugly Cottonmouth was already looking straight at me. I could have dropped into the water near the rock, but I didn't want to do that because I'd be defenseless against the snake which could bite me from the rock or, worse yet (if there was any worse) come after me in the water. Mary Lou was crying a little, softly, and Ben whispered to me to hold on tight. I did hold tight and jackknifed my legs up. The snake scared the piss out of me and I could feel the urine running down my leg. I was sweating too—from the heat and, especially, from fear. And, because I was sweating, the palms of my hands were wet and slick so that after three or four minutes, while Ben was thinking what to do, my sweaty hands began to slip on the vine and I descended very slowly. My arms ached something fierce with the strain, and I thought they were going to break off at the shoulders. I scrunched up my hands as tight as I could, but kept slipping down until I was a few inches from the level of the now fully alert snake, which had begun to coil even tighter. I knew I couldn't hold on much longer and my eyes teared in terror. I tried not to look at it, but I couldn't turn my eyes away from the snake which looked like the very Devil himself, the Devil Paps sometimes talked about. I was sweating badly now, shaking and aching and praying and afraid I was going to die. A split second before I fell into the water and hit the bottom running, Ben threw his hatchet and cut the snake clean in half. They told me later that the half of that horrible snake with the mouth at the front end was still wiggling as it slid off the rock into the water. I saw none of this because I was yelling and screaming and struggling to get out the water. I got out of the creek as if it were on fire and ran up the path toward home. Passing Ben, I saw that he was wiping sweat from his now pale face, breathing heavy and looking like he was going to be sick.

That was the last summer we cousins were in Georgia together. Ben went on to become a professor of electrical engineering at Georgia Tech. The girls both married lawyers. Billy was an automobile insurance adjuster until he got lupus and retired early. Once at grandmother's Billy got chiggers and poison ivy, both at the same time, on his you know what: his private. But that's another story.

As for me, I'm a writer. I take my grandchildren to the Bronx Zoo sometimes, but if they want to see the snakes I wait for them outside the Snake House. Snakes are awful. I really hate those fuckers!

With Ed Curran's father, Cliff, and my father, we cut wood for the fireplaces. One evening the chimney in our house caught on fire and the firefighters had to come and put it out. Also my mother made me take piano lessons which I resented because I wanted to be outside playing with my friends. I never got good at the piano. On one occasion my father asked me to put up the storm windows with him. I didn't want to so I had a temper tantrum and cried and cried. But I ended up helping him put up the windows. After a while we moved to a smaller house in Sea Cliff Sea Cliff where I shoot frogs in the pond at back with a BB gun.

My father was conservative with his money. My first job, for instance, was putting together sections of the Sunday paper at our local drugstore when I was thirteen. After three Sundays of this I had made ten bucks which I spent on two new colorful T-shirts. My father was most unhappy. My mother told me Dad thought I should have saved the money. But I didn't have enough clothes, which was typical. Later, when I went to a preppy college, I didn't have a suit and asked my father for money for one. Instead, he sent his cast off robins-egg blue zoot suit, which was the opposite of preppy. A zoot suit! With its outrageous baggy pants, long knee-length loose-fitting coat, and extra-wide lapels! In addition, my father was several inches taller than me so that it didn't fit as any kind of suit. Okay, our father was tight.

The Bicycle

One morning, on my eleventh birthday, after my father had gone to work, Mother told me to look in the garage. I did, and found there a splendid brand new bicycle: a maroon Schwinn "Challenger" bright and shiny.

It was a spectacular bicycle, like a Harley-Davidson without a motor: heavy and resplendent with chrome, it shone and glinted proudly in the sunlight of the open garage. I had never seen such a bike: it had wide white-wall tires on a sturdy body, a fancy chain-guard, a back seat over the rear wheel, a tough kick-stand, a big, comfortable leather seat with two shock absorbers beneath it, a horn in the middle of the frame encased in a streamlined canister stenciled "CHALLENGER," handlebars which angled high and had red plastic streamers flowing out of them, chrome fenders reflectors at the ends, silver-painted hubcaps, shock absorbers at the front wheel and an elaborate headlight above it. I was overcome, flabbergasted. And I convinced Mother to keep me from school that day so I could ride the bike.

We lived in a sort of housing development in these days, though a nice one. And it was moderately hilly. I took off and rode up and down these inclines, circling the neighborhood many times that day. The bike was very stable and easy to ride downhill, gathering its own momentum as it went. But uphill was pretty hard going because the bike was so heavy and had no gears. Sometimes, going uphill, I would have to get off and push my beautiful bicycle.

I had friends in the neighborhood and we spent a lot of time together, playing stick-ball or kick-the-can; but mostly just cruising around on our bikes, sometimes having impromptu races. My friend's bicycles, none of them new, were all just frames and wheels, light and made for going fast. And while my new bicycle was the envy of all, even though I was a strong and wiry kid, discovered after about a week that I simply couldn't keep up. The heavy bike was a lot of hard work.

So one day, after school, when there was nobody at home, I went into the tool box at the end of the garage, took out pliers and a couple of screw-drivers, and proceeded to dismantle the bike in order to make it lighter. I took off all the accessories and non- essential parts: light, horn, chain-guard, reflector, fenders, hubcaps, and backseat, along with their nuts, bolts and screws, and placed them neatly in a corner. Then, when he had just a frame and wheels, I went riding. The bike was lighter, faster, not as much effort, and I could now speed up hills.

My father was a mild-mannered, undemonstrative man who rarely expressed his anger. And he would hardly ever address his displeasure directly to me or my sister. We always heard from our mother how Dad felt about things. "Your father thinks you should study harder.

Your father is annoyed you didn't mow the lawn this week." Etc., etc. Our father sulked.

Anyway, when our father saw dismantled bike ("dismembered" he probably thought), he hit the roof. I heard Mother and Dad arguing furiously about me and about the bike for nearly forty-five minutes. Then my father went back into the garage, gathered up all the loose parts of my once beautiful bike, put them into a cardboard box, and threw them, one by one, into the shallow pond just beyond our backyard. Then Mother told me to go to bed early. Which I did.

After several days, I waded into the pond and retrieved every one of the bicycle parts. The pond was cruddy with mud, rotting leaves and branches, insects, refuse of all kinds; it was a filthy job. But I washed all the parts down with the hose, wiped them dry, oiled them, stored them under my bed, and never put them back on the bicycle.

Dad never talked to me about that beautiful and expensive Schwinn, and I rode the frame for years. As an adult, I keep the old bicycle parts, still shiny and wrapped in oilskin, on a shelf my garage.

Lament

My father never pranced me,
As some dads fool around;
He never read me stories nor wrestled on the ground.
He never really hugged me
Nor kissed me on the cheek,
And he so seldom listened that I could barely speak.
Now he's gone forever
And we don't have a chance
To sing a song together
Or swirl in loving dance.

Overseas

When my father was transferred overseas to run the operation in London and be chief Pilot there, it was too late to get me into an English School that year so my parents sent me to the French speaking part of Switzerland, to Lausanne on Lac Leman. I was fifteen. At the Lycee Jacquard everything was in French all the courses: chemistry, math, physics, etc. So I didn't learn anything except French. I roomed with an English boy whose feet really stank because he never changed his socks. And there were student boys from everywhere: Iranians, Italians, Germans, Arabians, etc.

One of the Germans was a bully, a bad kid, but a good tennis and ping-pong player. We played tennis against Le Rosey, a first class international school, established in 1880, which educated distinguished Royalties including the Aga Khan IV, Prince Rainier III of Monaco, David Niven, John Lennon and many others.

The Tennis Match

Günter is a pig. He has small, brown squinty eyes, pasty white skin, is stocky (a little flabby), and is somewhat less than medium height. He combs his thin brown hair like Hitler, straight across to the left. Günter doesn't like Americans, nor the English, nor, I suspect, anyone from the allied countries who have defeated the master race in the late war. Günter issues threats to us, in low tones, in the hallways of the Lycee Jacquard in Lausanne, Switzerland where I am at school for a year. Once I saw him beat up a tall Italian kid from Milan. My roommate, Lewis, is a proper English boy whose feet stink because he wears his socks for three or four days at time. I am fifteen. At the Lycee I learn French but nothing else, except to avoid Günter, who is eighteen and mean.

Günter is an excellent table tennis player. He tells us he is the junior ping-pong champion of Munich. He probably is. Nobody at school can beat him.

It is spring of 1953 and we have an athletic meet against another nearby boys' school, Le Rosey. "the school of kings," is one of the most exclusive schools in the world. It caters to the dynastic royalty of many countries including those of the Middle-east and Egypt, to rich South American families, to the Rothchilds, the Radziwills, and to the progeny of Hollywood stars and business magnates. At this time the future Aga Khan is at Le Rosey, as well as the son of the then CEO of Coca Cola, a son of a American NATO general, and Prince Rainier III of Monaco. Our school, the Lycee Jacquard, is more middle-class.

The tennis matches between the two school teams are played during other events, but the final match, between our number one player and theirs, is the highlight of the day. The match interests me because I have played number five on our team and lost, as have our numbers two, three, and four. Günter is our best player; he is squared off against an American named Troy.

I know guys like Troy. He has gone to Choate or Exeter and is taking an extra year at Le Rosey to learn French. Most likely he lives in Darien or Greenwich, Connecticut in a big house. His mother is beautiful and speaks through her teeth with her lips closed in an upper class accent; his father is an investment banker in New York with Morgan Stanley, or a partner in another prestigious law firm. Troy's sister is beautiful too. The family hangs around the Country Club pool or tennis courts in summer and skis in Aspen in the winter.

Troy is a picture book tennis player, an all-American boy: tall, tanned, blond crew-cut hair, lean but muscular, apparently fast and agile. In the warm-up, his strokes are so smooth and impressive that it is obvious that he has been taught well and at considerable expense. He hits the ball hard and decisively, both backhand and forehand, volleys with ease, and seems to have a very hard serve. Troy plays a power game and radiates electricity and enthusiasm for tennis.

Günter, on the other hand, hits the ball with unimpressive slowish pace and serves the same way; he appears nonchalant, his play seems lackluster. It seems to me this match it will be no contest.

They play on an all-weather hard court. Troy wins the toss. He throws the ball high on the first serve, reaches for it, and whips his arm down from the elbow, like a hammer. The serve is a boomer, an ace straight down the middle. Fifteen-love. The American moves to the left, bounces the ball a few times, lofts it, brings his feet together, reaches up, and hits another hard one. Out. The second serve is hit with pace also, but somewhat slower and with side-spin. It bounces high to Günter's forehand and is returned across court to Troy's forehand. The two players trade several baseline shots until Troy hits a blistering forehand to Günter's backhand and moves swiftly to the net. Günter's return is only a moderately high lob which Troy goes up for like a basketball player for a rebound. He smashes it for a point. Thirty-love. Troy hits another hard serve and, with three long strides, attacks the net again. Günter returns it down the middle and Troy angles his volley out, missing the sideline by half an inch. Thirty-fifteen. Günter returns the next serve with an undercut spin which just goes over the net to Troy's backhand. It is a difficult touch shot, dangerous if not played perfectly, which it is not; Troy volleys it cross-court for a winner. Forty-fifteen. Troy serves another ace and wins the first game. Günter's face gives nothing away.

The hard-hitting, serve and volley Australians dominate the first ranks of tennis in the 1950s. Lew Hoad, Frank Sedgman, Ken Rosewald Rod Laver, and John Newcombe are our heroes, along with the American star Tony Trabert. Theirs is the kind of tennis we want to play: serve hard, rush the net, volley crisply, and sledgehammer the overheads. And when on the baseline, hit out for the sidelines. To us it is high risk, masculine, exciting tennis; the only way to play. Troy plays like that. Günter decidedly does not.

Günter is a mystery. Why is he such a perverse creep? Is he conflicted his sexuality? Some of us have girlfriends, or ogle girls at the Ouchy waterfront on weekends. But Günter doesn't seem to care about girls. What are the sources of his anger? Maybe his father was an infantry officer killed by an American bomb. Did Günter experience the fire-bombing of Munich? Günter is too young to have been a member of the Hitler-Jugend, but he must have belonged to and been indoctrinated by its feeder group the Nazi Jungvolk which took boys from ages ten to fourteen. These youth groups emphasized athletics, discipline, and hierarchy. And certainly Günter had seen the ubiquitous last official photograph of The Fuehrer taken outside his beleaguered Berlin bunker on April 20, 1945. It shows Hitler reviewing a small group of uniformed Hitler Youth and awarding them Iron Crosses. This image sticks in the minds of Germans, particularly of German youth, for many years afterward.

It is hot and bright. this afternoon. Troy continues to play his big, energetic game and wins the first set six-three. Patterns are emerging. Günter is a retriever. He plays steady, cautious, conservative tennis, rarely goes to net and almost never hits the ball out of court. His ground strokes, forehand and backhand, are solid and usually hit with topspin. Yet he can employ a variety of others spins, lobs and undercuts. Whereas Troy, as I have said, plays the then orthodox strongman game, the extreme game. Troy's facial expressions and body language reveal his pleasure in the game: a slight smile, a balled fist after winning a rally, a tap of the racquet against his thigh, a light skip after each game won. Günter is utterly impassive, expressionless. Except once when the umpire calls a good shot, a liner, out: Günter glares at him and shakes his head in disgust.

When Troy returns to the States in late June he will probably be given a Corvette as a graduation present and he and his childhood girlfriend, Missy, a very shapely blonde whom he will marry after business school, will spend a lot of time cruising around in it. Missy will go to Vassar and Troy will go to Yale where his father and grandfather matriculated, or maybe to Princeton. He will play on the tennis team there and belong to Scull and Bones or an equally exclusive fraternity or eating club.

All tennis players talk to themselves. What do they say on the bench after the first set? Troy: "This guy is steadier than I thought, but doesn't hit for winners. He plays a dinks game. I can overwhelm him, out muscle him. I'll keep coming to the net. I **am** tennis!" Günter: "He's good, strong, but a little erratic. I can wear him down physically, tear him up psychologically; he'll make mistakes."

Günter serves the first game of the second set. His serves are accurate, if not fast. There is little difference in pace between his first and second serves. And because his first serves are almost always good, he has little need for a second serve anyway. Yet he can spin his serves several ways. Günter serves one ace during the entire match: a twist serve to Troy's backhand which hits the line. Nearly all of Günter's serves and ground strokes stay in.

Günter loses the first game of the second set and Troy loses the second, although both games are close. One game apiece. During this set, Troy will serve four aces, Günter none. Troy returns Günter's serves with hard, flat shots which often hit the sidelines or baseline. Günter returns Troy's drives with deep, rather slow strokes which always land an inch or two inside Troy's baseline, often near the sidelines. While Troy's shots are either in or out, but usually by inches, Günter rarely hits the lines because he, intentionally, does not shoot for them. It is becoming clear that Günter has excellent hand-eye coordination, good patience, and first-class court sense. He is an unlikely looking athlete, but will show great determination and will reveal superb, almost uncanny anticipation. Except for Troy's service aces, Günter can make a good return off of nearly all the American's shots because he is, most of the time, in exactly in the right place on the court. Despite Troy's pace, Günter's returns are not just defensive push-backs, but offensive strokes. "I can run him from side to side and tire him out," he says to himself. And Günter takes full advantage of the sun, lofting beautifully placed lobs which Troy, not sighting them well, often miss hits or pounds out of court. Troy, on the other hand says to himself: "I'm the better athlete and in better condition.

I'll keep pounding the serve and rushing the net. I'll keep the rallies short by volleying. He'll get discouraged." But Günter doesn't get discouraged; fed by Troy's increasing errors he gets stronger, looser, and more confident. "I'll show him," he says. "I'll cut this American rock star down to size."

Günter has unusual finesse. Once in a while he makes an under spun chip shot which passes low over the net. Troy rushes in to take it and more often than not, punches the ball out of court or into the net. Günter himself only comes to the net three times during the entire match, both times after deep lobs into the sun. And each time he makes one of the most difficult tennis shots of all, a drop volley. A drop volley takes the pace off your opponent's ball and places it low and just over the net. This truncated stroke is done with under spin so the ball drops flat and, rather than bouncing forward, comes to a stand-still. The drop-volley takes so much touch to perform that it catches Troy completely by surprise each time. Once Troy fails to get to the ball, once he hits it into the net, once he angles it out of court. Günter wins the second set seven-five. At the end of it both men are perspiring profusely. Günter wipes his face and changes his shirt.

It is hard to think that Günter will allow himself to be taken up by the craze for American jazz, rock and roll, and frenetic dancing which will invade post war Germany and which is considered by many Germans, as well as their church leaders, decadent and dangerous to the prevailing conservative ethic. It is more likely that Günter will look upon this kind of rampant individualism as barbarian, anti-German, and disgusting. More likely, with a gang of neo-Nazi cohorts, he will bully and threaten those who embrace the music, films and manner of American culture. I see Günter in the future as a brooding minor government functionary who lives alone and plays tennis and ping-pong as often as he can. He will probably belong to some ultra-conservative secret society. But who knows, really, where his brand of determination will lead him.

Troy is worried as he walks a little stiffly back onto the court and steps up to serve in the first game of the third and final set. He knows he has played okay in the previous set, but not well enough. And he puts so much more energy into the game than Günter (or so it seems) that he's is getting tired faster. "What to do? Serve and volley, of course. And settle down. I'm the bigger, better player. I can still blast him off the court." But this kind of self-talk does not work for Troy. Günter, meanwhile, thinks: "I've got him now. He's tensing up; he'll start making more errors." Troy keeps hitting hard and Günter keeps returning well-placed shots deep into the opposite court, first to one corner than into the next. He keeps Troy running from side to side on the baseline. Troy is getting discouraged. And the more tired and discouraged Troy gets, the steadier and more accurate Günter becomes. He senses he is going to win. He sees Troy weaken, he smells blood, he's a bloodhound going for the kill. The score is now three-one in favor of the German. The match had turned.

Spectators usually thin out during a long tennis match, but by the middle of the third set, word has spread around Le Rosey that their tennis star is in big trouble. It is approaching supper time and many of the other athletes have showered and changed. More come to watch and the crowd builds.

Troy is very nervous now. His unhappiness shows in his face and high anxiety forces him into jittery errors. It is his turn to serve and he does so knowing it will probably be one of his last efforts. He serves two aces in the fourth game and wins it. Three-two. Günter is confident, at the top of his game. He exhibits an even icier calm and in this set has made no errors whatsoever. He knows he can win. His accurate serves are harder now and land from side to side in the service box. Günter is loose, relaxed. Troy miss-hits Günter's serves or hits too many of them out. He is getting desperate, he is falling apart, he has slowed down. His schoolmates urge him on but he cannot rise to the occasion. It is five-two, Troy's turn to serve. He serves an ace. One-love. He hits three first serves out and his second serves are hesitant, weak. Günter returns the serves deep, with perfect placement, and wins each rally. Five-forty. Troy double faults for the match. He is desolated, destroyed. Without shaking hands with his nemesis, Troy walks off from the court looking at the ground. Günter takes a little bow as he thinks "Deutschland uber alles!"

Günter is a hero for two days and takes compliments with a surprising degree of grace. On the third day, however, he is a pig again, his usual arrogant, insufferable self. I see him accost a small boy in a hallway of our school. And I walk away.

I shoot hoops on the basketball court when I didn't have classes and for three months in winter the school moved to Zermatt where we went skiing from eleven to four-thirty. At other times we would sit around and listen to the big bands; somebody played the clarinet and he was good. Everybody wanted to sound like Benny Godman. We had one pretty good skier, an English boy whom I later saw on the British ski team in Kitzbuhal. But their team was not much good and no match for the Austrians, French and Germans. It was at the Lycee Jacquard that I meet Guy de Vincent, a young man who was the Belgian junior speed skating champion. We went skiing together and one day he was following me down a fairly difficult slope when he fell and broke his leg. I felt very badly about that. I visited Guy in England where his parents had sent him to live with a family to learn English.

At Zermatt I meet a pretty girl from Venezuela who went to a girl's school close to the Lycee Jacquard. But she was young and pretty well supervised. Back in Lausanne I snuck out one night and, hiding in the bushes, I went to meet here at her school. We embraced, but nothing really ever came of it.

Of course I learned to swear in French, not really knowing what the words meant. And I learned to love Toblerone which I still like, and I got drunk on wine by myself at a local café. I remember going to the laundry and responding to a question about when I wanted

my laundry back with "Je mon fou" which meant I don't give a fuck.
I then left Switzerland and attended the English school Brighton
College. Brighton was only a moderately good school, but it has since
become first class.

At Brighton I continued with French, studied Shakespeare, and
had to be tutored in Algebra and Geometry. My tutor was a tall man
with yellow teeth and bad breath. Tutoring didn't do much good;
I've always had to struggle with math. But in the British system, if
you understood the principal of the problem you could demonstrate
that principal and still get a good grade without getting the correct
numerical answer. I also learned to play rugby and squash. In rugby
I played on the first team, usually at fullback, because I had very
good hands and could catch anything. I got my school colors after
the first season. I also played tennis and was on the tennis team, as
well as snooker which I could never win. One very windy day Mal
Henry, a short fast friend, set the world's record for the hundred-yard
dash. The track was downhill and the wind was blowing hard behind
him. The boys who couldn't do much else, who were not athletes,
had to do cross country. I used to watch them come in and throw
up. Later, during a spring break Mal, Rob Hartley, and I went to
Paris and visited a night-club where Mal, who played trombone well,
played with the band. Another time John Wallace, Rob Hartley and
I went on a trip to Scotland. We drove in my father's Studebaker and
stopped, one night, at an inn in Liverpool. John made off with the
housekeeper and he wanted to keep it quiet. But when he came back
into the room the bed fell down and woke everybody up.

At first we stayed in a dorm. Tony Bennett was my roommate
in the second year. Tony's mother owned a pub downtown to which
we scurried off on weekends and sometimes spent the night. We had
to be careful of the Teddy Boys, gangs who dressed in Edwardian

clothes and who would beat us up and steal our hats if given the chance. Tony and I were fast friends. After rugby matches we shared two to a bathtub and once a week we had our own single bathtubs. Larry Weathersby, an American, who the next year went to Yale and became a well-known doctor, was at Brighton on an Anglo American Exchange scholarship. He took me aside one day and said I had fallen in with the wrong crowd—referring to some boys from London who I hung out with. They weren't particularly bad, just kids who had some rough edges. The next year, John Wallace came over on the same scholarship. It was John who convinced me to apply to Princeton where he was going.

On a spring break I was strolling about in Piccadilly Circus on the way home when a man approached me. He said I was so good looking, like a movie star and that if I came home with him h would feed me dinner and fix me up in the movies. I didn't go with him but when I got home I told my father and mother about him and my father was furious. The man was gay of course.

I was at Brighton College for two years and took the O level exams. The headmaster didn't want me to leave. He wanted me to stay another year and take the A level exams. He said I was too immature to go to college.

But go to college I did, applying to Harvard, Dartmouth and Princeton. I didn't get into Harvard or Dartmouth. I think these schools got the same applicants and said "you take him, I'll take him, and you can have O'Neal. I don't think I'd have a chance of getting in to Princeton these days: there are too many smart Asians and women.

At Princeton I roomed with John, and down the hall were three persons from Atlanta: Ivan Allen, Tread Davis, and Mason Lowance. We brought them a bottle of whiskey and found them holding a prayer meeting. The next year we had eight roommates and stayed together for the following three years: the aforementioned from Atlanta, Chris Fishbacher, a Swiss, whose father owned a 200 year old textile business. John Oster (of "Osterizer" fame), Phil Becton, Mike Lanham, A. W. Karchmer, John Wallace, Dick Brennen, and I. Three became lawyers, two became doctors, Oster and Fishbacher ran businesses, one became a college professor, and Phil Becton and I joined the Army Flying Corps and the Marines respectively. Brennen died of cancer, Allen committed suicide, and Lanham had a heart attack. The rest are still living.

In those days, grades were posted on a bulletin board, for all to see, in McCosh Hall. I had taken psychology expecting to read Freud and Jung and the like. But it was a statistical course, Pavlov's rats in a maze and I my first grade was a five (lowest- a failing grade). My friends all said goodbye to me, "it's been good to know you". But my next grade, In French, was a one (the highest), so I hung in.

I majored in French Language and Civilization and eventually graduated with a gentleman's average (a 3). Oddly I never stuttered at all in French. I think you take on a different persona, a different personality when you speak a foreign language and are able to hide your disability within it. I wanted to ask many question in classes but didn't do so because I was afraid I'd stutter. Princeton is one of the few universities that require a senior these for all who want to graduate so I wrote on Cezanne, in French. My thesis advisor was Maurice Coindreau, William Faulkner's translator. I admired him because Faulkner was extremely difficult to translate. He translated **As I Lay Dying** for instance as **Tandis Que J'Agonise.** I also took Italian with a professor who was such a good teacher that he never published anything.

My fondest memories of those days were playing rugby. I truly enjoyed rugby. Three of my roommates also played: A. W. was hooker, Phil Becton played in the line, John Oster was second row in the scrum, and I played either fly-half or fullback because, as I said, I had very good hands and a decent kick. In our senior year I was elected co-captain, mostly because I knew the rules. But Don Morrow my co-captain, who played scrum half, was a better captain than I. I was too indecisive. Many colleges didn't let their football players play rugby because they might get hurt. Some of the Princeton players went to Bermuda during spring break to participate in a rugby tournament, but I didn't have enough money to go. Also in our senior year we went undefeated by beating Dartmouth which did let its football players play.

> O the pleasure I've had from games well played
> Played hard to win on fields arrayed
> With teammates brave and unafraid:
> Companions of my youthful days
> When we in glory were all ablaze.

> Hands that caught the ball are gnarled and veined.
> Eyes that sought the instant break now ache.
> Legs that ran the field are sometimes pained.
> And feet that zigzagged fast are not so fleet.
> This mind that called the plays knows better days.
> And ears that heard "Well done!" fade one by one.

> But when I sleep and dream, O the glory of it all:
> I'm back upon the field and will not yield.
> When games replay within my head in dreams
> I'm with bold-hearted friends who made the teams.
> So when in these dreams I often recall then
> And think about we young and stalwart men—
> Ah! The pleasure's double sweet, twice as sweet to me again.

A circus came to town which had a small elephant. Mason Lowance and I decided we couldn't graduate without feeling the elephant's balls. So we did. And there was an incident I didn't feel good about in retrospect. A young woman from California came to Princeton to be with me for a special weekend and I dumped her into the hands of someone else. Years later I wrote her and apologized for my crass behavior.

I met Ernest Hemingway, when at Princeton, in 1959 and wrote about it much later:

Drinking with Hemmingway

The skiing was good the day before we met Hemingway. It had snowed all day and the going was sometimes hard. But we were young and wiry and strong and had skied well in spite of the snowstorm. The snow was soft and the falling down was part of it and the skiing was good.

Doug Bradshaw, Tim Houghton and I were juniors at Princeton. We had come to Sun Valley to ski during Christmas vacation. The Bradshaws lived in Pocatello but had a cottage in Ketchum a few miles from Sun Valley. Doug and his brother Ben, and their St. Bernard, Fritz, and Tim and I shared the Bradshaw's cottage. Tim was from Vermont and was the best skier among us. He was eccentric too. He was a sort of wild card and skied on the edge of control. Tim majored in English and was taking creative writing from the British novelist Kingsley Amis who was a visiting fellow at Princeton that year. Tim admired Amis and when he graduated he went to London to study under Amis. Shortly after he arrived in London, Tim died there in an apartment house fire.

Hemingway had been renting a house in Ketchum that fall from the Heiss family. The morning after the skiing in the snow storm, which had been good, Marge Heiss called Doug and said that Hemingway was leaving her house for the last time. If we hurried, we might intercept him. We got in the car and drove to the Heiss' old log cabin which was covered with snow.

Hemingway came down a narrow path cut between five feet of snow on each side. He filled the space and was cradling four bottles of Wild Turkey Bourbon. Not one bottle, not two bottles, but four bottles. Hemingway looked like a grizzly bear. Just like in his photographs. He must have been warned and was not surprise to see us. We were slack-jawed by the great writer but somehow got introduced all around. Hemingway asked us for a ride to his own house on the other side of town which he and his wife Mary had just moved into. We were dumbstruck at this turn of events but piled back into the Bradshaw's Chevy station wagon. Doug drove and Ben was in the front passenger seat. Tim and I flanked Hemingway and his whiskey bottles. Fritz rested his slobbering head on Hemingway's shoulder.

It was eleven in the morning and snowing lightly. Hemingway was in a festive mood. He said we should stop at the Tram, a local bar and restaurant, where he would buy us all a drink. We parked in front of the Tram and walked to the door. It was closed. Hemingway said "Fuck it. Let's go to my place." As we all walked back to the car a young bug-eyed professor hailed us down and Hemingway invited him to come along too. Doug drove and momentarily lost control as the car skidded around a corner in the fresh snow. Hemingway said "Damn good slalom turn."

Mary was not home and Hemingway said "Where the hell is Mary?" She was not home so Hemingway made the Wild Turkey drinks and told us they were "the best goddamn drinks you'll ever have." The drinks were strong, especially in the morning, and they were good. Hemingway stood in the living room because, he told us, he had a back injury from a plane crash in Africa years before. We knew that Hemingway wrote mostly standing up. We could see his tall desk in the adjoining study. Mary came home before long, with Taylor Williams, and she took over the bartending. Her drinks were strong and good too. She must have been used to making strong drinks for Hemingway.

We four young men were wise enough and polite enough not to ask Hemingway anything about his writing. Or we were scared to ask. Not so the young and callow English professor who we found out taught at Northwestern. He asked a couple of silly questions to which Hemingway did not reply. Then he referred to *Across the River and Into the Woods*. Hemingway said "For Christ's sake it's *Trees* not *Woods*." Undaunted, the professor then asked something about Henry Morgan in *To Have and Have Not*. "I never answer that kind of bullshit," said Hemingway.

Tim did ask Hemingway about Carlos Baker's book *Hemingway: The Writer as Artist*. Baker was a Princeton professor from whom Tim took classes. "It's all fucked up," said Hemingway. He said that Baker thought Jake Barnes' sexual frustration in *The Sun Also Rises* was because he had had his balls shot off. Hemingway said Barnes had had his "cock shot off. His cock, not his balls. Now that's real frustration." Then he advised us never to make an important decision or enter an important contest or sporting event without first getting laid. "It clears the head and concentrates the mind," Hemingway said. He said we should never take the advice of a Catholic priest because "anyone who doesn't get laid can't be trusted to give good advice." Hemingway then retreated to the door of his study with his friend Taylor Williams.

Taylor Williams was a hard-drinking skirt-chaser twelve years older than Hemingway and was Hemingway's hunting and fishing guide in and around Sun Valley. Hemingway liked Williams and admired his skill as a guide. The two friends had known each other for years and Williams sometimes visited Hemingway in Key West and Cuba. They were good friends. Hemingway was a pallbearer at Williams' funeral in 1959 and was buried next to Williams in the Ketchum cemetery.

We listened to Hemingway and Williams talk of the Battle of the Bulge. Hemingway had been in the battle as a war correspondent and Williams had lost a son there. Hemingway said the U. S. Army

Officer Corps was caught completely off guard when the Germans advanced. "The battle was one big fuckup," Hemingway said. "One big fuckup." He said "for a while the brass had no goddamn idea what the hell to do." Hemingway and Williams talked about the war for some time. By that time we were drunk and couldn't keep up with the conversation so it was time to leave and we said goodbye to Hemingway and to Williams and to Mary, thanking them for the time and the drinks, which we thought were real good, and staggered out the door into the snow which was still falling lightly and slipped around a little bit before falling into the car and somehow Doug drove us back. We were too drunk to ski that afternoon. Meeting Hemingway was good, real good. The drinks were real good too.

My family, my mother and father and brother Steve, went to Kitzbuhel, Austria, for skiing during Christmas for three weeks along with a bunch of other Pan American pilots and their families. I flew from New York, sub low of course (paying passengers first) After about four days waiting at the airport, I went back into New York and stayed at a flophouse near Penn station. It cost fifty cents and the rooms had ship-like doors which banged shut. In the morning the near homeless passed around a razor in the bathroom. But I finally got on a plane and then took the train to Kitzbuhel.

There I met Jean-Pierre Dijon (Jacques) who, about my age, who was from Paris. We played bridge, had meals together or with my family, went out at night, and so forth. By then my French was pretty good and I could pass for French if I didn't get into a philosophical conversation or talk about mechanical engineering or anything atrociously deep. While in Kitzbuhel I saw a friend from the Lycee Jacquard practicing with the Great Britain team but Great Britain could not compare with the Austrian and French skiers. I also saw an American woman miss a turn on the Hahnenkamm (a difficult piste and the site of the World Cup). She hit a tree and later died in the hospital. Many of the ski instructors had been in World War II and some had lost arms or legs. But they skied anyway on artificial limbs and were very good. I went to Jacques' family home later on and we went to Zermatt together to go skiing. In Zermatt we met a couple of girls and I learned a valuable lesson from my friend: if you want to get laid always choose the less attractive one. He did and got laid, I did not and didn't get laid.

I met my wife Mary at a party in New York. It was a coup de foudre for us both and we made out in the bathroom almost immediately. We were gone before her date arrived. I shared a room at Princeton with

---

After college, Princeton arranged for me to go to France to Cement Lafarge a cement company for the summer, ostensibly for a management position at the factory. It was in the Maritime Alps north of Nice at a place called Contes Les Pins. We worked from seven to twelve then took two hours for a large lunch with wine. Very little work was done after that before stopping at four. I drove around in a new Renault Dauphine, obtained in Paris, which my father had gotten me for graduation. I made friends with a Frenchman and his family who lived close by and I corresponded with them for a while afterward. My French got better and better.

I finished that summer by going to Cannes and sailing for a month, on a fifty-five-foot yawl, in the Mediterranean. We went up and down the coast and to Majorca. It was my roommate Chris Fishbacher's father's boat. There were me, Chris's girlfriend Analese, the father, Chris's brother, and two young women. One of them became Theresa Heinz, who, when Senator Heinz was killed in an airplane crash, became one of the richest women in America and married John Kerry. It was an idyllic and thoroughly relaxing experience.

The Marine Corps

I was in the Marine Corps from September 1960 to September 1963. At first it was more training at Basic School in Quantico, Virginia, then to Camp Lejeune in Jacksonville, North Carolina. I told Mary, who later became my first wife, that I wanted to finish Basic School before getting married. But that idea dissolved and we got married a month after I got to Quantico. We were married in the Westside Church in New York and the minister had the nerve to ask us if we were getting married there for the prestige! It was a very small wedding: me and John Wallace as best man, Mary and her sister as bridesmaid, my mother and father, and Mary's mother. My father thought I was too young to marry and that I was marrying below my station. He was very unpleasant, sulked, and went to bed at nine o'clock.

A. W. Karchmer who was an excellent student and studied late. When he returned from the library Mary and I were often in the room with the door locked. This made him mad as hell!

At graduation our senior year I went parachuting and so did Mary. We practiced landing by jumping off a table a few times. Then we went up in a small plane and jumped off of a static line, of course at about 2,500 feet. I jumped first, Mary second. There was a target in a farmer's field and I was able to hit it by using the risers. Mary, however, couldn't steer so she disappeared into a corn field and sprained her ankle. She had never been up in a plane before and for some time afterward she said she'd gone up but never landed.

I enlisted in the Marine Corps because I didn't know what else to do. Between my junior and senior years, I went to Platoon Leaders Class. You were supposed to go six weeks between sophomore and junior year and six weeks the following summer, but, along with my friend Walt Smyth, I did twelve weeks in a row. The training was vigorous to say the least, but not without humor.

"Ho, Ho, Hey, Ho
One, Two, Three, Four
United States Marine Corps
One, Two, Three, Four
United States Marine Corps
One,
I can't hear you
Two
A little louder
Three
Get it together
Four
A little louder
One, Two, Three, Four
United States Marine Corps
Oorah, Oorah
United States Marine Corps"

When Bud, who was in the middle of the column, passed out on the Hill Trail, in full field gear, we heard him clanking all the way down the left side of the hill. Later we awarded him the uncoveted Wimp=Out Prize for fainting. George Lewis had fainted four times in four weeks and had consequently garnered the most points toward the prize. But it was the spectacular dive of Bud Lee that summer, perhaps the all-time greatest faint ever, that immediately won him the prize: a quart of Jack Daniels and a bottle of Vitae smelling salts.

On no evidence other than our own biased opinions, we thought it was the hottest summer on record at Quantico, Virginia. And our combat gear raised the temperature by at least ten degrees. Some of us, particularly those from the northern states, passed out now and then: during field maneuvers, on the obstacle course and, especially, at formations on the parade ground. We were told not to lock our knees while standing at attention, although a loose stance didn't always help. Ingestion of salt tablets helped us fend off dehydration, and we constantly drank water, beetle juice, milk, coffee, whatever.

We dreaded the Hill Trail over which we were required to walk, trot or run on forced marches with full equipment: 45-pound pack, rifle or BAR, K-bar, canteen, helmet, and other military paraphernalia. Our drill sergeant's name was Ferlingetti. He was short and trim and always impeccably turned out. He was all spit, polish, and curses. He called us "maggots". Taking his lead, we called him maggot behind his back.

First Lieutenant Brown, the CO of our training platoon, was tall, skinny and mean, with bad teeth and an albino-like complexion. He resembled a ferret and had the cruelest mouth and smallest eyes I've ever seen. We were glad he was not usually directly involved in our day to day training. If he or Ferlingetti didn't like you they made you a runner on the Hill Trail. A runner was placed at the head of the column with the Lieutenant and had to relay messages from him back to the sergeant at the rear. Ferlingetti would then give the runner a return message to deliver to Brody at the front of the column. The messages were always chicken shit such as "What do you think we're having for chow tonight?" or "What was John Wayne's greatest role?" or "Do all Marines eat bullets?" In this manner the runner had to cover twice as much ground, or more, as the other marchers. Especially if the column was really strung out. If you were designated a runner, the grinding routine could set your head spinning and your heart pumping wildly.

The twelve-week Platoon Leader Class determined which of us would become Marine Corps officers. Some flunked out for lack of leadership, some for poor physical fitness, others couldn't take the harassment, and some just quit and went home. One of our troop, from Canada, who had done six weeks the summer before, never opened his foot locker so that when he arrived that summer his and gear were moldy and mildewed. He was immediately washed out.

Bud's real name was Beauregard Madison Lee. He had brown hair, blue puppy dog eyes, and a mild manner to go with his drawl. But he was fit and muscular, had good military bearing, was usually ship shape—except after a weekend on the town—and was not easily riled. Bud went to The Citadel and was descended from several distinguished Virginia families. His uncle had been a Marine General in World War II and his father was a United States Senator. Consequently there was no way he was going to be washed out of basic training. We knew this, so Bud bore the brunt of many pranks.

Sergeant Ferlingetti drilled us hard and subjected us to great verbal abuse. He was an artist at insults and had a verbal style which presumably he had perfected for the enlisted men as a D.I. at Paris Island. Of course, we were all enlisted at this time, not receiving our commissions until after we had graduated from college. Ferlingetti yelled at us all, together and individually, and his language was often foul. His favorite word was "maggot," followed by "shit bird," "fuckin' weenies," "momma's boy," and "mothafucka". Although few of us realized it at the time, "maggot" was actually a word of affection for recruits. He constantly told us that we were maggots who had shit for brains and no balls; that we were worse than turds in a toilet bowl and weren't fit to wipe the asses of real Marines. Before each weekend liberty he'd dismiss us with: "Those army wimps may have R & R, rest and relaxation, but I know you boys are going for the Marine Corps version, I and I, intercourse and intoxication. So don't come back with the clap or worse." And Ferlingetti was an unlikely poet who could improvise raunchy cadences instantly:

"Your mother's a lush and your sister's a whore
One, Two, Three, Four
"You can't go back, your home is the Corps
One, Two, Three, Four

Under these dismal boot camp conditions, it was important that we leavened the hard, crusty bread the Corps was determined to make of us with humor.

Beauregard Madison Lee was a spit shine poster Marine, well-built and ruggedly handsome, and his gear was always squared away, especially his boots which were highly polished. We all wore the same boots and several of us had extra pairs. One morning when Bud was in the head, we hid his left boot and substituted another right one for it, the correct size and equally polished. Bud noticed the switch, of course. But when it is time to fall out in Marine basic training, it is time to fall out on the double—with no ifs, ands, or buts. So that morning, during close-order drill, Bud was limping and hobbling to Ferlingetti's ringing cadences as best he could. Since a Marine's feet are of utmost importance, we gave Bud his boot back at a smoking break after the drill.

One day during a field exercise, John Babbitt, a candidate from New Jersey, found an old M-1 rifle under a bush at the edge of a swamp. It had been a dry year and the swamp had less water in it than usual, yet it was clear that the rifle had been submerged for a very long time. The bolt and other works were rusted tight, the barrel was stuffed with crud, and the wooden stock was rotten and pitted. We were married to our M-14 rifles ("If the Marine Corps wanted you to have a wife they would have issued you one.") and had to fall out for head count and rifle inspection every morning before breakfast. When Bud was asleep we exchanged the cruddy M-1 for his shiny M-14 so that when reveille sounded at 6:00 he had to fall out with the only rifle available to him. I won't tell you everything Sergeant Ferlingetti said when he came to Bud in the line but it began with "WHAT THE FUCK..."

Like the rest of us, because we were always so tired, Bud was a very sound sleeper. So about 11:00 PM one night, when Bud was

soundly snoring, six of us easily detached his upper bunk from the
one below it and carried it quietly onto the parade ground. The next
morning, when the bugle blew reveille in the dark, Bud awoke outside.
Ferlingetti found him, in his skivvies, near the door to the barracks
dragging the bunk behind him. Our drill sergeant's reaction can't be
told, but it is said that he had a smile on his face.

Another trick we played on Bud was to insert an empty clip into
his rifle so that when the command to "present arms" was given at
formation the clip shot up into the air at least five feet. Bud always
checked his rifle for an empty clip after that, but several others in our
platoon were victims of this ploy.

On another occasion, Jake "Cowboy" Hitchings filled Bud's
canteen with grog. Hitchings, a Texan, who had served time as a
navy seaman, was the oldest recruit in our platoon, and knew some
naval history. Grog, equal parts of rum and water with sugar added,
was served in the old British navy. We went on a field maneuver that
day, clearing enemy house to house in the wooden training village set
up at Quantico for that purpose. The "enemy" was another platoon
and all of us were firing blanks. The exercise commenced in the early
afternoon and ended about four hours later. Early on, I saw Bud take
a swig from his canteen, choke, and spit. But, since the whole platoon
was in on the joke, no one would give him water. It was hot, as usual,
and Bud, who was well known for being able to hold his liquor, had
no choice but to drink from his canteen between periods of frenetic
action. As the day wore on he became quite mellow.

The grenade was my idea. In retrospect it was a bad one. Over the
top. In the seventh week of the twelve week course we were introduced
to the hand grenade. Everyone in the platoon threw a dummy grenade
first to get used to the timing and motion. The dummy grenades were
real but with their powder and detonators removed. Then we hurled
live grenades over a shoulder-high wall into a sandpit. I managed to
conceal an extra dummy grenade in the back pocket of my fatigues.
That night we placed the grenade, with the firing pin pulled almost

all the way out, in Bud's bunk just below his pillow. When Bud curled back the covers on his rack, he jumped and let loose a string of oaths which would have made Sergeant Ferlingetti proud. Bud railed at all of us in no nonsense stentorian tones. "I've had it with you stupid sickos," he shouted. "Any more crap like this and I'll beat the shit out of you all, one by one!" Next morning, when his anger had more or less subsided, Bud made it clear, nonetheless, that he had had enough.

The next week someone came up with the idea of messing with Bud's gas mask for the run through the tear gas chamber, but we decided against it.

Beauregard Madison Lee made a fine regular officer. He was a Captain in Vietnam, led an infantry company, and received a superficial wound. After twenty years in service, Bud retired and became CEO of a middle-sized office supply company in Richmond. I saw him recently at a reunion in Quantico of our Basic Officer's School class. We laughed about the things that happened to him that long ago summer.

Over beers, Bud and I told each other a few jokes. Such as the one about the two green second lieutenants who were walking down town together in Jacksonville, North Carolina, home of Camp Lejeune. One said "Where did you get such a great bike?" The other lieutenant replied "Well, I was walking along yesterday, minding my own business, when a beautiful woman rode up on this bike. She threw the bike to the ground, took off all her clothes and said, "Take what you want." The first lieutenant nodded approvingly, "Good choice; the clothes probably wouldn't have fit."

Then Bud told me about something that happened in his infantry combat training and jump school at Camp Pendleton. A new officer, he said, was assigned to lead a platoon of parachute qualified Marines in a practice night drop. The drop zone was to be lit by orange smoke. As the plane flew toward the drop zone, the officer was trying to see the ground features and locate them on his map. Suddenly he saw a lot of smoke ahead. The smoke was black, not orange, but assuming it to mark the right place, he gave the order to his men to jump. When all had safely exited the plane, the officer jumped too. On the way down he heard groans and curses from his men, accompanied by a foul smell that got worse as he descended. He had jumped his platoon over a garbage dump!

At Basic Training School the routine was still rigorous but not as hard as the Platoon Leaders Class. We studied Marine Corps history and traditions, *The Art of War* by Sun Tzu, field tactics, how to form a defensive perimeter, rife drill and other such stuff. And, of course, there was the ubiquitous Hill Trail. The most embarrassing thing happened to me in the Corps. We had to give a field lecture about anything: Marine Corps discipline, how to field strip a rifle, how to set up a defensive position, and so on. When it was my turn I went blank and couldn't say a word. Put yourself in my shoes and imagine not being able to speak to a hard-assed platoon of officer candidates! My father didn't think I would make it in the Marines. In typically indirect manner, he told my mother who told me. It was the only time I was glad my father didn't speak directly to me.

Mary and I lived in a gatehouse on an estate in the countryside in Warrenton, Virginia. We broke champagne glasses in the fire place, a Marine tradition, and invented a game which my uncle got patented for us. We also went to dinner at a retired Commandant of the Marine Corps house for dinner. Aside from the work, and the inevitable shinning of shoes and boots, it was very pleasant. We were there for about three months. When graduation from Basic School was reached, we were recruited, for future jobs, by the CIA, IBM, the FBI and similar organizations.

While I was at Camp Lejeune, Mary and I lived in a small town called Swansboro about ten miles from the camp. There was a wooden gate at one end of Swansboro, and not long before 1960, the gate would be closed except of Thursdays when the Negros could come to town. On a monthly salary of $275 per month we couldn't afford much. We rented a house from Captain Pete who also ran a fish restaurant. The first house was extremely shabby; the second house was right on the water and water spilled into the living room at high tide; the third house was better; at least it was on dry land and had three bedrooms and one bath. This last house backed up to an inlet off the Intercostal. We had a small boat ad went spear fishing for flounder at night with a lantern at the bow. There were wild ponies on islands in the waterway and we got pleasure from that. We also went surf casting on sandy islands off the coast. We'd get surf casting rods from Special Services and stick them out the sunroof of our Renault. We'd bait the hooks with shrimp and never knew what we'd get: blue fish, flounder, and mackerel. In one instance we caught a pompano and took it to Captain Pete's to see what it was. It was a delicacy he said and told us how to cook it. We also went bottom fishing getting into the ocean through a small rough break in the islands; the captain drank brandy and Mary and I got sick. I started a newspaper, *The White Oak Scene* in Swansboro, which must be very rare because it lasted only a few issues. I also drank Southern Comfort with Bill Noe, a catholic priest who was assigned to our small town. Mary and I and Walt Smyth went out to the Black Beach, a beach where Negro Marines sunbathed and swam. On the way out the ferryman told us not to stay very long; we were clearly not welcome there. A few weeks later we saw a tornado come right up the street in Swansboro.

At Camp Lejeune I became a Language Officer and ran the Second Interrogation/Translation Team. There are two such teams in the Marines, the other at Camp Pendleton in California. We taught basic interrogation techniques and military terminology so we could translate documents and learn the enemy units and strengths.

We used native speakers from Canada and Puerto Rico or South America and we had a Russian speaker who had gone to the Monterey Language School.

The Taking of Fort Royal

We saw the boat from a long way off motoring, under bare poles, slowly down the center of the Intercostal Waterway. As she drew closer we could see the sails were neatly furled. The skipper brought the blue and white sloop Mirabelle, about forty feet long, slowly to the small dock. As he glided her in single-handedly, we saw he wore a battered straw hat with two miniature Budweiser beer cans on it and a red and yellow plastic flower between them. Below this he had on a colorful Hawaiian style short-sleeved shirt outside of blue and yellow checkered shorts. He was swarthy and tan colored. I stepped to the end of the dock.

"Need any help?"

"Thanks," he said, throwing the coiled bowline across the water to me. I tied the bitter end of the line off on a cleat. Then he moved aft and handed the stern line, over the ever decreasing gap between boat and dock, to my wife who tied it off on her end. After we had together rigged fore and aft spring lines, the skipper turned off the engine and invited us aboard.

"Want to have a look?" he said.

So we hopped on.

It was September 1960. I was serving in the Marines. We lived in Swansboro, North Carolina and would often go to the town dock in the evening to see if any interesting boats came by. Swansboro was a very small town, with no proper Marina or refueling facilities, and while we often saw nice boats pass up or down the waterway, they seldom stopped or overnighted.

He told us his name was Jorge and that he was bringing the boat north from Fort Lauderdale to Norfolk, Virginia for the owner who wintered it there. After we chatted for a while he invited us to go up the waterway with him. That seemed like an excellent idea, but Mary and I wanted to know him a little better, to make sure he was safe, not a nut case. So we invited him for dinner.

After a few beers and then some hamburgers, our guest seemed reasonably sane so I called my CO and he gave me Monday and Tuesday off. We looked forward to a long, adventurous sailing weekend. Then we took Jorge spear fishing for flounder. We had learned that if the night is too bright the flounder are easily spooked and hard to get, and if the water is not calm they are hard to see. But this night was perfect for flounder: dark with just a sliver of moon, and calm. The yard of our little rented house backed up to an inlet off the waterway and we had a small flat-bottomed skiff. We attached a lantern to the skiff so it hung over the bow and illuminated the water below it. Then two of us poled very quietly in the shallow water where flounder came in to feed while the third kneeled in the bow, spear at the ready. When we were over a flounder, a sharp, quick jab would get it. If the jab were too slow or clumsy, the flounder would scoot away. The technique takes some practice. We took turns spearing and after about an hour and a half we had each bagged a big flounder. We took them back to the house, Mary and Jorge cleaned and boned them, and put the fish in the freezer. Then Jorge went back to the boat.

The next morning Mary and I went to the dock with a few clothes, some food, a bottle of gin, and some tonic water. It was early but Jorge was ready. He started the engine, I threw the dock lines to Mary who was on deck and hopped on myself as the Mirabelle gathered way.

It was a pretty day and the scenery up the waterway was enchanting. We passed farms, timberlands, fishing villages, hardwood wetlands, wide vistas of marshes and cypress swamps, grasslands filled with birds, big beautiful houses, cottages and shacks. Often we stuck close to the shore so as to better see the sights. In this way we saw an alligator slither off the bank and a bobcat sitting on a tree limb. We also saw the occasional falcon, hawk or bald eagle. About noon we passed an island on which we spied, through the brush, a group of small wild horses. As we motored along, the vegetation included, juniper, pine, honeysuckle, wild grapes, and Spanish moss, and we passed several large boats going south as well as a kayak and a party of canoes.

I wanted very much to turn off the engine and sail but we were in narrow waters and Jorge was on something of a deadline, so we motored all day up Bogue Sound. We passed Beaufort, then into Core Sound, then, just past Smyrna, we found an isolated picturesque cove to anchor in. Before dinner of hot dogs and salad, we broke out the gin and tonic for Mary and I. Jorge drank beer.

Jorge was a first generation Cuban who lived with his girlfriend Teresita, a restaurant hostess, in South Miami. They had a one-year old son about whose antics he told us with delight. He thought he and Teresita were going to get married soon. He had longish black-hair and brown-eyes, was well-built but not fat, about six feet, and quite good looking. He was cheerful, smiled a lot, and was a good companion. Jorge was swarthy, brown but not black; it was as if he had a permanent tan. He had the radio tuned to Latin American music most of the time. Our skipper was thirty-one and well-enough known as a reliable delivery captain. He told us he could usually get as many jobs delivering boats for the wealthy as he wanted. Then, from wherever he ended up, he would take the bus back to Miami. He liked being on the water okay but said it was lonely work. Which, presumably, was why he had invited us along. When not driving boats, he worked at various odd jobs such as cleaning fish, construction work, and drugstore security.

After that first day, I wanted all the more to get into wide water where we could sail, so I convinced Jorge to set off early on Saturday morning. We left about 5:30. By 10:00 we were passing Cedar Island and breaking out into Pamlico Sound. Pamlico Sound has a north-south axis and is about ninety miles long and thirty miles wide. Nowhere more than fifteen feet deep the sound is often much shallower. When sailing there it is important to keep a constant eye on the depth finder. But it was a beautiful day and the sailing was great. Even better in the afternoon when the wind came up and blew ten to fifteen knots. We saw other sailboats, fishing boats and, particularly, crab boats lowering or taking up their pots. With the motor turned off it was quiet and peaceful. I knew how to sail pretty well and Mary was a good first mate. When Jorge understood that, he had enough confidence in us to take a nap. At one point, after getting to the western coast of the sound, I wanted to explore a river which was entered under a draw-bridge. Lulled by the fine sailing, I wasn't thinking straight at that juncture. We approached the bridge under full sail going about four knots. I assumed the attendant would see us coming and draw up the bridge. But the bridge didn't budge and we were getting far too close. When I frantically sounded the canned emergency horn, Jorge woke up and came charging on deck. He quickly lowered the job and mainsail, turned on the engine and put the boat in reverse. We came to a stop about fifty yards from the bridge which still wasn't opening and Jorge looked at me with frowning trepidation. We didn't go up the river, but headed back out into the sound and our skipper stayed on deck most of the rest of the day.

It was beginning to get dark when we got near Fort Royale and Jorge wanted to anchor near the shore again. As we approached Fort Royale, which was nothing more than a country club, a small Marina, and, we later saw, a gated residential community, Mary and I wanted to stop there for the night to get showers and a good meal. The food we had been eating was okay, healthy enough: carrots, dried fruit, cereal, bread. But it was not tasty. I saw some empty slips on the dock and suggested to Jorge that we stop.

Jorge, with a strange expression on his face, was quick to answer: "No, I can't stop here."

I explained to him why we wanted to stay but he just shook his head, somewhat sadly.

I said, "Why don't you want to? It would be nice"

"I really can't," Jorge said.

"Why not?" I insisted.

"Well, because, you know, this is the south."

Mary, always perceptive and empathetic, understood before I did. She gave me a look, and then it dawned on me: Jorge regarded himself as black, or whites regarded him as black, and he had undoubtedly been turned away from such places before. As for us, Mary was from New York and I was brought up in Connecticut. Neither of us had any real understanding of southern life-style or culture. And since the Marines were fully integrated, I had no experience of racial prejudice. We were hardly freedom fighters, and we were naïve. It hadn't occurred to us that Jorge would not be welcome at Fort Royale. Besides, he wasn't even black, not by our definition. The three of us sat in silence for a while as we got closer to the berths. Finally, I used all my persuasive powers to get Jorge to tie up there and ended by saying something like "We'll do it together, we'll be with you."

Looking forlorn, Jorge reluctantly replied "Okay, but you'll have to be the owner."

A man we assumed was in charge stood on the dock peering at us through binoculars. We were close enough by then to hail him with our bullhorn, and identified the boat by name, gave our place of embarkation, and asked if we could have a slip for one night. "Who's the captain?" the man said, looking skeptical.

"I am," I replied.

The man helped us with the dock lines, then, still looking at us disapprovingly we felt, collected the berthing fee and walked away.

Jorge was gloomy at the whole prospect of being there and made it clear he wasn't going to dinner with us. But we introduced him to gin and tonic, strong ones: in his glass more gin than tonic. This tactic lifted his spirits somewhat and we convinced him to eat at the Country Club. I gave Jorge an extra short-sleeved dress shirt with collar that I had brought along to go with a pair of khaki pants he fished out of his duffle bag. Then we went to shower. After showering we three walked toward the clubhouse. We kept talking to Jorge but he walked stiffly, as if he were going to an executioner, or a lynching.

The clubhouse was a large white building with a cupola, or widow's walk, on top and a big front porch with fluted columns. The place reminded me of the master's house of an ante-bellum plantation, and I half expected to walk past slave quarters. We approached it, in the dark now, via a long driveway lined with palm trees, and it was no doubt an especially long walk for Jorge. There were a few cars in the circular driveway, including two Mercedes, a Porsche and a Cadillac. The double doors opened to a wide hallway beyond which was an expansive dining room.

The startled maitre d', whose eyebrows lifted visibly when he saw us, was in black tie. Mary was a beautiful young woman in those days, a head-turner, and she is still very attractive. As the maitre d' led us to our table in a corner, heads did turn but not, I'm sure, just to look at Mary. We glad to at last be seated. It was a relief. We noticed then that the other diners were mostly well-dressed and that we were the youngest guests by several decades. We ordered Cabernet Sauvignon to go with the roast duck stuffed with a crab, baked potatoes whipped and put back into their skins, and butter beans. For desert Mary and I had strawberries over ice-cream; Jorge had chocolate-mousse. The waiters and waitresses were black and while our waiter was very proper, there was a twinkle in his eyes and a hint of a smile on his face. Parts of the kitchen staff kept gathering in their doorway and gaping at us. Then they retreated and other staff took their places. The other guests pretended not to stare, but they did. They spoke in hushed tones and we were sure their conversations were about us. Even though Jorge noticed all this this, he was pretty looped and had a good time, not to speak of an excellent meal. We left a generous tip. In the end we were pleased to have conquered Fort Royale. Being in no hurry to get underway the next day, we left the dock mid-morning and had a fine sail up to Englehard. There Mary and I said goodbye to our friend and we returned to Swansboro on the bus.

We got invited one evening to a party by the late illustrator and children's book author Wesley Denis who wrote about horses. Denis lived on top of a hill. It was raining and I got drunk. When leaving I turned the wrong way and got stuck halfway down the hill. We got a tow truck to pull us out of the mud the next day. Another time my wife and a friend were driving from Swansboro onto the base when the car turned completely over and both women got out through the open sunroof. Someone called me on the phone and said my wife had been in an accident, then hung up. For days before getting the car fixed, I had to drive with my head sticking up out of the roof. The sentries must have had a chuckle when they saluted me that way.

We hunted for books and other things in antique shops in and around Swansboro. I had a book, *Gold in Your Attic*, which listed rare books and their values. I remember finding a copy of Robert Penn Warren's *The Circus in the Attic and Other Stories*, 1947. It is one of the most difficult titles of Warren to find in a dustjacket and was really the start of my career as an Antiquarian Bookseller.

As a First Lieutenant serving a three-year stint in the U. S. Marine Corps, it was all a game, something to do after college before getting a real job. The field exercises, the rifle range practice, map reading and orientation, the forced marches, the assaults on bogus enemy, the mock amphibious landings, the howitzer training, and all the classroom work on leadership, history of warfare, and Leatherneck values and customs—these things were just part of a big war game. I liked the neat uniforms, especially the dress blues and his officer's ceremonial sword, as well as the frequent giving and taking of salutes. And I liked his gear: rifle, pistol, knife, canteen, bullet pouches, helmet, web belt, and other military stuff. Now and then Mary and I drank and danced at the Officer's Club, went fishing on the Outer Banks, or sought out antique shops.

In Jacksonville, North Carolina, at Camp Lejeune, it was nice and warm and friendly and pleasant, and there was nothing going on. It was peacetime and peaceful, not at all war-like. At twenty-two I was fresh out of college and newly commissioned as were most of the young officers with whom I trained and socialized. I knew something about Marine Corps history: Bellow Wood, the Pacific Islands Campaign, the fighting retreat from Chosen Reservoir. And I'd seen a lot of war movies starring Steve McQueen, John Wayne and others. Intellectually I knew what war was; yet in my gut, in my heart and soul, I really knew nothing, I had experienced nothing. I was just participating in war games in North Carolina.

War Games

On top of this, what made the illusion even greater, what made the idea of combat less real was that I taught school. Because I spoke near fluent French, I ran a language school for turning mostly French and Spanish speaking Marines into translators and interrogators. It was a cushy job which I enjoyed.

The linguists at the Interrogation-Translation Team were mostly enlisted men from Puerto Rico, Mexico and Central America, or French Canadians. These native speakers were taught elementary interrogation techniques and military terminology in their respective languages.

I particularly liked two of the French speakers, Staff Sergeants Richardson and Lavau. Both were relaxed, congenial, confident men, middle-aged, well-built. They were good-looking, square-jawed recruiting-poster type Marines. Richardson, from St. Louis, had gone to the Navy Language School at Monterey; Lavau was from Quebec. Both had been in Korea, but he never heard them speak about it. The school ran smoothly.

Then one day the Cuban Missile Crisis. Warrant Officer Davis got the phone call from G2. He went outside to where I was chatting amiably with my two sergeants and passed the word to the three of us. Richardson's hands began to shake so much he spilled most of his coffee; as Lavau wiped sweat off his forehead, fear showed in his brown eyes. And so it was that I found out, from battle-hardened warriors, what was real. As we waited we studied up on Cuba and finally went to Morehead City where we boarded and LST. The Landing Ship Tank is a flat bottomed ship and, with no stability, gets tossed around a lot. Most of us slept on deck and got very sea sick. When we got back, I asked Davis, who had learned Russian at the Monterey Language School, what happened. His mission, he said, was to translate between the captains of the American blockade ship and the Russian ship coming to Cuba. He was terrified he was going to say the wrong thing and start the Third World War!

I played on the Fleet Marine Force soccer team against the Navy in Norfolk, Virginia. We had one terrific player, a young man from Brazil who played center forward in the front line. But the rest of us were not so hot and the Navy beat us eight to nothing. That may have been because I was playing defense. And we just couldn't get the ball to our center forward. I had better luck playing tennis with the general's aide.

Here is a poem I wrote, years later, at the first reunion of my Basic School class:

In Memoriam
Written for U. S. Marine Corps Basic Officer School 5-60, First Reunion, June 2004.

They were our classmates, these fine men;
we often do remember when
we marched with them in well-pressed greens
and learned to be fighting Marines.

We trained as leaders, they did too,
and fought in fields we never knew.

They were brave and they were strong
in a war which soon went wrong.

They were the best of all the rest
when they were put to combat's test.
We knew them well, it's sad to tell:
they went, they fought, and then they fell.

Those whose lives were swiftly riven
died with pride, that's a given.
They were good men, we say out loud,
"They were our friends, they made us proud."

They are all heroes, these fine men,
now we remember them again.
They were warriors and Marines,
we see them sometimes in our dreams.

Their bodies lie in Arlington sod,
their souls have gone straight up to God.
We'll go there too, we still firm few,
and say to them, "God bless you."

They led Marines in jungle greens
and gave no quarter, so it seems;
so when we meet them up on high
we will salute them—"Semper Fi."

*

For those captains killed in action in Vietnam: Ronald Gregory
Babich, Frank Pierce Kolbe, Kenneth J. Howard, Leo Joselane III,
Robert Francis Morgan, Richard Frank Wallace.

Just before I left the Marine Corps I got very depressed and they called it anxiety. My uncle, a lawyer, got me a thirty percent disability which gave me about $300 per month. At that time, I wanted to be a journalist and had a choice either to go to journalism school at Columbia or the University of Missouri. I choose Missouri. Not because I was afraid of the academic work or the competition, but because I was afraid of living in New York.

In Missouri I studied for a couple of weeks before I got so depressed I could no longer work. My wife arranged a flight to Berlin where my parents lived. We got there and in my depressed state I read all of the James Bond novels in a week. Then I went out into the woods and slit both wrists. It was a cry for help. I saw a psychiatrist a few times then went to England where I was deposited in the Priory, a mental institution.

The Priory was just outside of London, a place where the glitterati went such as Eric Clapton, Kate Moss the famous model, and Douglas Badger, the World War II ace who flew with both legs amputated, and other people. I remember, especially, an American who had Tourette's syndrome. While eating dinner she would suddenly shout, in a strident voice, "pass the fucking butter" or "give me the goddamned salt". And of course, like many patients, I was infatuated with my young Hispanic nurse. At The Priory I first had ECT (electro convulsive therapy). I had it several times. In those days sodium pentothal was used to knock one out and large paddles were used for the ECT. Mary visited me every other day.

The Priory didn't work very well so I was sent to McLean Hospital near Boston. My father accompanied me and I was put in the maximum security building. I begged my father not to put me there and cried and cried, but I went anyway. It was a dark and creepy place and I stayed there for a couple of weeks.

I was then transferred to another more congenial dorm. In this place we had real silverware and real plates and napkins and the food was quite good. I met Gordon (Gordy) Howard there, a Harvard graduate about twenty years older than I. Gordy, good looking, was a character and must have been drugged up because he would dance on top of the tables. Meanwhile Mary lived in an apartment in Cambridge and visited me most days. As I got better, I actually went skiing with a friend I met at McLean, and I won the tennis competition on a nearby court I could see from my window. James Taylor the singer and the poets Robert Lowell and Sylvia Plath also sojourned there and I remember a veterinarian who would or could not move and had to be carried from place to place by two aides. I had several psychiatrists.

My first psychiatrist was Dr. Peter Jenny. He was a kind and compassionate man. I don't remember the name of my other psychiatrist but he was also nice. McLean was perhaps too good a place. It had great lawns in rolling hills and a building with a commissary where eventually I was allowed to go unattended. Dr. Jenny got a job as psychiatrist at MIT and I saw him there several times. The play *Hair* came to MIT in the summer. It was a blast and disrupted the campus and students danced in the street with little or no clothes on. Dr. Jenny had purchased a Porsche. I told him not to feel guilty about it and he chuckled. Eventually I got somewhat better and left McLean to join my wife in her apartment in Cambridge.

I attended, several times, the Manic-Depressive Society meetings which were held in a building on the Mclean Hospital grounds at night. The meetings were dark and dismal and we broke into groups and discussed medication, coping strategies, and other things. The people who had it worse were the rapid cyclers who went way up and way down in the same day or less. We had a lecture on Prozac which said that people could die from taking it. When I thought about this, my take on it was that very, very depressed persons didn't have enough energy to commit suicide. So they took Prozac which lifted them up and then they suicided.

I was playing tennis with Gordy when my son Stephen was born. Stephen had colic. One day he swallowed something and almost died. We rushed him to the hospital in a panic. He threw up just as we got there and everything turned out okay.

Afterward we lived on a big estate in Milton, Mass. The house was built by Captain Robert Bennet Forbes of China Trade fame. We were custodians and curators and lived on the third floor. It was a fascinating place and was jammed full of interesting stuff, such as several copies of Nathaniel Bowditch's translation of Laplace's *Mecanique Celeste*. I was writing during this time and got a job boiling down the news for a neighbor's business. I would read the news and paraphrase it. We entertained there quite a bit. The alarm was motion sensitive and the wind was always setting it off. I had a big stick and would go down the stairs. One evening the Forbes's had an exhibition of China Trade Silver gathered from the family and posted a policeman to guard it without telling me. The alarm went off and I went down the stairs with my stick while the policeman went up. It was scary when we met!

John Van E. Cohn of the legendary Seven Gables Bookshop in New York called my first catalogue "one of the best first catalogues he'd ever seen." It had two unrecorded books of American poetry, one printed in Kennebunk, Maine in 1819 and another Wilmington, Delaware1785, several James Fennimore Cooper novels in original printed wrappers, which are rare, and a book by George Henry Calvert presented to Poe. And I became known initially for private press and printing history.

We also bought, from an institution, a collection of about 1,200 items relating to world's fairs, 1850 to 1900 and sold it to a university. We bought and issued as our catalogue 20 the *Phelps Collection of American Almanacs* beginning in 1679 and containing 2500 almanacs. This catalogue has been chosen to be among the 100 best catalogues of the 19th and 20th centuries, principally because no one had devoted this much time to almanacs. It was begun by Azor Phelps who was a pallbearer at George Washington's funeral.

And strange things happened in the rare book business. For instance, I wanted to be an analytical bibliographer and had gone to Simmons College at night to get a Master's degree in library science. While there I appraised four incunabula which are books printed before fifteen hundred in the "cradle of printing" which had begun in 1450. Shortly thereafter I got a phone call from a young man saying he had some books for sale. I recognized the titles immediately and called the police. The cops said to meet them at a hotel in the suburbs and one of them would pose as my client. I did so and we went to the young man's apartment. A policeman and I went up the stairs and one waited outside. We didn't know if he had just these books or many others. It turned out he had only the four. He had a girlfriend at Simmons and just took these books one day. He was arrested and I was on the news that night. Another time the rare book librarian at the Library of Congress offered us some books and we made an appointment with him. We saw that the books were stolen from the library and called in the FBI. The books were first edition of Joseph Conrad's novels, were quite valuable, and were clearly marked with the Library of Congress stamp. The FBI arrested the man in our office. Still another time we appraised a collection of books, the property of a deceased woman, which she had given to the Boston Athenaeum, an old subscription library. There was one very good book: a seventeenth century book on animals illustrated with marvelous copper engravings. A few days later a young man called and said he had a book for sale which I knew right away was the book I had seen. I told him I knew it was stolen. In this case I told him to give it to the Boston Athenaeum. He said he lived in the same building with the woman and took the book on a whim. On another occasion a women called me up and said she wanted large size folio cover for her dog to sleep on before the fireplace. As it happens I had one which had some old prints in it. I took the prints out and sold her the cover.

And another day a real estate magnate said he wanted some old sets, which looked somewhat shabby, for his library. The sets I had were in fine condition and not suitable. But I went around an gathered up sets which were worn and soiled and they fit the bill.

I got very depressed for a week and drank so much whisky that I got the DTs and shook and trembled so hard that I had to go to the hospital again even though I tried to convince my psychiatrist that I was okay. Another time I got crazy manic and with typical super abundant intelligence and confidence, I fixed the telephone which had been bouncing around from our office to our home and back. I was awake all night, went out to the esplanade overlooking the Charles River and eventually my family had to barricade the front door so I couldn't leave. In the morning Mary took me to Massachusetts General Hospital, kicking and screaming and refusing to take a shot of Haledon. But eventually they gave it to me, then they transferred me to a hospital in Salem, Mass. After I was there for a day, I pretended to have been with the CIA, put my hands up in a defensive position, and told them I had some moves that could really hurt them. The aides left me alone after that.

In Boston a rather scruffy young man came to our shop saying he had for sale a collection of "airplane books" garnered from a private collection. This turned out to be a fabulous collection. There were lighter-than-air and early heavier than air items, pamphlets, broadsides and books. The books were about early ballooning by the Montgolfier brothers, Jefferies, Wise, Monk Mason, Blanchard, Lanza Turzi. and many others; also books by the Wright brothers, Eiffel, Langley, Lindberg, Lilienthal, and other pioneers, and some very strange flying machines: the Ornithopter, a bird like flapping-winged, flying sea-going vessels that were paddled through the air, balloons supposed to be navigated by strange sails, the Dragonfly or Reactive Passive Locomotor, the Aervolante, and so forth. It was truly a great "airplane" collection which we sold mostly to Virginia Polytech which collected such thing s for NASA.

Our catalogue 126 was devoted to science and was based on the collection of George Wald, a Noble Prize winner in biochemistry, and contained many off-prints of Wald and other famous scientist. It had books and papers on aeronautics, biochemistry, biophysics, computers, evolution, neurophysiology, philosophy psychology, physics, astronomy, technology, and vision. It also comprised the work of forty-four recipients of the Nobel Prize.

We also put out a catalogue, in gold and black, of *Black History* which was a major success. And yes, we bought 18th and 19th century pornography and eventually sent it to auction in Germany. Germans love that stuff. Within a space of two years we acquired two good collections of French books: the first was a group of first edition, in nearly mint condition, limited and signed of Camus, Mauriac, Celine, Sartre, Anatole France, Jules Romain and others; the second was books by Francis Carco, the collection amassed by his friend and biographer. Carco wrote exclusively about Paris, it's cabaret life, art and music, and contained many good illustrated works and limited editions. We sold both collections to an American university. One day came a handful of good old books on shells. And we also got a collection of early American tune books which were duplicates from an institution. And we brokered the letters and manuscripts of Henry Knox who was George Washington's Secretary of War. This great collection is now in the Pierpont Morgan Library in New York. One of the last things we did was to seek books sold to Congress by Thomas Jefferson. These books became the foundation of the Library of Congress. There were initially about 6,000 volumes and over the years two thousand or so had been lost, stolen, mutilated, or destroyed. We got the exclusive contract from the Library of Congress to supply these books and came up with about 1,200 titles in several years. If, for instance, Jefferson had an edition of Cicero's *Orations* printed in Venice by Aldus Manutius in 1578, we had to find that exact edition. And since Jefferson was a Francophile, the project put my language skills to good use. One of the last things I did as a book dealer was to buy a broadside from a doctor was also dealt in books and broadsides. It was a rare printing of the American Constitution, 1788, and I bought it for $75, held it for a while and then sent it to auction where it brought $75,000! I can assure you this was highly unusual. I split the profit with Mary and left for San Francisco where my oldest son, Steve, lived and my youngest, Mason, was soon to follow.

I got very depressed for a week and drank so much whisky that I got the DTs and shook and trembled so hard that I had to go to the hospital again even though I tried to convince my psychiatrist that I was okay. Another time I got crazy manic and with typical super abundant intelligence and confidence, I fixed the telephone which had been bouncing around from our office to our home and back. I was awake all night, went out to the esplanade overlooking the Charles River and eventually my family had to barricade the front door so I couldn't leave. In the morning Mary took me to Massachusetts General Hospital, kicking and screaming and refusing to take a shot of Haledon. But eventually they gave it to me, then they transferred me to a hospital in Salem, Mass. After I was there for a day, I pretended to have been with the CIA, put my hands up in a defensive position, and told them I had some moves that could really hurt them. The aides left me alone after that.

The Boat Trip

January 6 and 7 1990

If we had known the sailing trip would be a near disaster, we wouldn't have gone. There were three generations of O'Neals. Ages about 9, 26, 35, 56, and Tad Stride, 11, as well as the Captain, Ted

Loughman, who was about 35. Young Steve and I were from New Ipswich, New Hampshire, my brother, Zaire, the Congo, my father, was from Guadalajara, Mexico, Tad Stride (my sister's son) was from Longwood, Florida.

The party arrived at the boat about 8:00 P.M., where the Ricki was berthed in Dania, Florida in a canal next to the home of the owner, Mr. Caldwell. After storing our gear checking provisions and equipment, we decided to leave prior to the scheduled sailing time of midnight. We left the dock at 10:35 P.M. and motored along various canals past Port Everglades and into the open sea at Fort Lauderdale. In order to get more favorable winds for the Gulf Stream crossing, to Bimini, we went south until abeam Miami before turning almost due east. Since, the wind was nearly calm and from the southeast, we soon realized we would have to furl the sails ad go to engine power if we wanted to dock at Bimini during high tide which was required for a boat of our size—a forty foot sloop. This was to be a health trip, according the big Steve the mate: no drinking, no smoking. But my father and I had brought some booze ad cigarettes and at the sign of the slightest trouble Steve broke them both out.

While most of us were sleeping, leaving only the Captain and mate on watch, there was suddenly a dead silence as the engine sputtered to a stop. After several unsuccessful attempts to start it, we decided to go back to Fort Lauderdale for repairs before continuing to the Northern Bahamas. Taking advantage of a following wind, we returned by sail to within a half mile of Lauderdale, dropped anchored at about 8:00A.M., and the captain rowed in for help. We waited about three and a half hours during which time everybody on the boat, except the mate suffered various degrees of seasickness. My son and Tad were particularly ill from seasickness and we laid them upon the concrete dock. They looked like they were dead but, eventually, little Steve asked for some ice-cream so we knew he was all right. By this time, we began to realize the boat was not in great shape!

At about 10:30 A.M. the rescue boat with Ricki's owner and two diesel mechanics arrived and we were towed to pier 66 at Fort Lauderdale. The engine was finally repaired and we were ready to go at 6:00 P.M. Since everybody had recovered from seasickness and was in far better spirits, we again sailed south to Miami and set curse for Bimini.

January 6th:

It was supposed to be a nine-hour crossing, but due to a flat calm, it took sixteen hours before we docked at Brown's wharf in Bimini straits. Each of us had made a bet as to what time we would arrive. The one with the latest arrival time won, and the mate had the latest arrival time. A couple of hours were consumed in feeling our way into port with a lead line because the approaches were shallow and we missed high tide by about three hours. We spent the afternoon and evening in Bimini cleaning up and getting ready for the next day's sail. We telephoned Tad's and little Steve Mothers to tell them "All's well."

January 9th:

We weighed anchor at high tide (10:00 A.M) and sailed south in the gulf stream past South Bimini, Gun Cay and Cat Cay, and anchored about 500 yards off South Cat Cay where we spent the afternoon sailing a trimaran which we towed behind the boat, swimming, exploring the island, and getting sea shells. Late in the afternoon the captain and mate (my brother, Steve) went diving for lobster among the coral off shore. They returned with five which we consumed for dinner in the form of lobster chowder. Then, early to bed after a busy day.

January 10th:

Another day pretty much the same as the 9th except that the captain and mate went spear fishing for an hour, using compressed air tanks for breathing. It was the mate's first dive and went off well, except that they got nothing with the spears so we had a fishless dinner. Later in the afternoon we decided to leave this delightful spot and headed south t a group of small rocks where we anchored for the night and did some more diving the next day. Soon after getting under way, however, we discovered that a fuel line ad broken. Ewe turned off the engine and headed north under sail for Bimini to make the necessary repairs. We had a couple of trolling lines out and just before arriving off Bimini we hooked a five pound fish which fought like a marlin for fifteen or twenty minutes marlin before we finally boated it . We had it for breakfast the following morning. A better meal is hard to imagine. The captain decided to wait until moonrise before proceeding over the shallows into Bimini proper so we anchored for a couple of hours a half mile offshore. By the time we arrived at the Bimini docks, and since the slips were already taken, we tied up for the night close to shore.

Shortly after dawn, a boat left the slip we had been waiting for so we docked in its place. Tad had decided the preceding night he had had enough so quick arrangements were made for him to fly to Miami and then to Orlando where he would be met by his mother. He caught the 9:00 A.M. ferry for South Bimini and the airport, and was badly missed the rest of the trip.

The rest of the morning was spent in various ways but in the afternoon the skipper produced a powered raft and three of the party took a ride around the straits which culminated in a visit to the Marine Life Laboratory where they viewed penned shark and fed a very interesting ad intelligent dolphin called Charlie. This was followed by a tour of the island by motor bike, supper, and a night on the town by the skipper, mate and Dave. They drank and danced until the wee hours.

January 11th:

Due to the "Night on the Town," it was midmorning before we started and headed south again. As the sea was too calm for sailing, we motored down, trolling unsuccessfully all the way, and anchored close to our old position off of South Cat Cay.

My son Steve and I spent the afternoon sailing the trimaran and collecting shells on the beautiful beach while the captain and mate went spear fishing again. Since they failed to see any fish, they settled for gathering about a dozen conch which were in the rocks and sand near the boat. By this time, it was getting late so we made preparations for conch chowder. Since neither the mate nor the captain knew just what to do, it took them at least an hour to separate three conchs from their shells and then we all went below to watch the preparation of the chowder by the mate who had been turning out gourmet for the entire trip. Many suggestions came from all corners as to what ingredients should be used and how the chowder should be cooked. The mate took the all good naturedly, following some of the suggestions, discarding others, and tasting frequently as he chowder progressed. When finally the big moment arrived, the stew was ladled out on top of a base of rice ad we all starting eating. All that is except the mate, also cook and sampler, who declined to serve himself and suddenly started roaring with laughter. Soon the others found out why. The conch was leather tough and was gritty with sand. It was taken out of the stew and thrown overboard. The rice, minus the conchs, wasn't too bad. We all went to bed early.

January 12th:

Another beautiful day like all the others so far. The captain and mate set of in the dinghy with their spears in hopes of bagging some game fish, but they didn't see any and concentrated on lobster instead. Big Steve got seven in short order so we were assured of a good dinner without having to open more cans. In the meantime, me and little Steve had sailed to shore in the trimaran and we all rendezvoused and spend an hour or so rowing, sailing and viewing the interesting marine life from the zodiac that the mate had brought along. Beside conch and lobster, there were many beautiful colored tropical fish staying close to the coral ledges.

We decided to have lunch ashore, so Dave went back to our boat for hot dogs that the captain had brought along for this purpose. By the time he returned we had a fire going and lunched on roasted hot dogs, beans and bead, washed down with Seven Up. By this time it was nearly four o'clock so we went back to the boat for rest and relaxation. While we rested, the captain, Ted Loughman, went for a long sail and returned jut as sunset, After a great dinner of lobster tails, we went to bed, still with a clear sky calm and gentle swells from the southeast.

January 13th and 14th:

Sometime after midnight the swells and waves became noticeably larger as the wind picked up. Sleeping became difficult due to the pitching and tossing of the boat (we were beginning to get wet also) and those who got up early noticed that the trimaran was missing. It had apparently parted company with the Ricky and was nowhere in sight. Most likely it had been carried away rapidly by the combined forces of the wind and the gulf stream and was no doubt headed for England.

After breakfast, we hauled up the anchor with considerably difficulty and headed across the stream to home port, expecting to arrive in the early evening. We sailed for a while but the boat healed over so much because of the rough sea that it became too uncomfortable. After trying a storm jib, we furled all the sails and motored the rest of the way.

The clouds were thickening fast and by noon we were in driving rain and wind of about 45 knots. We all got extremely wet and no one slept, but no one complained, not even little Steve. About ten miles from the Florida coast we went through a cold front and the wind shifted to the northwest for a time, but had no effect on the towering seas which had been building up for hours. Our spirits rose upon sighting the coast but fell again when we could not pick out any recognizable landmarks in the awful visibility. My father, who was an airline pilot, tried the radio. It could receive but not transmit. Believing ourselves to be off Miami, we turned north and paralleled the coast toward what we thought was home port. Then we made the error that was to cost us another eight hours in that terrible sea. All the time we were parallel to the high swells which made rough going for the boat and its occupants who remained miserable and soaking wet.

After heading north for about an hour we realized that we had already passed Port Everglade so we reversed course a hundred and eighty degrees and returned south. We continued in a southerly direction for two and a half hours, passing a solid line of high rise buildings and finally sighted several red and white lights on the horizon. Thinking they were channel markers for Port Everglades we continued on in the raging storm trying meanwhile to sight a liner which had run aground off Port Everglades. The mate was steering while the captain and Dave kept a lookout from the cockpit. Suddenly the skipper yelled for 10 degrees reversal of course because he could see the outlines of a reef ahead which stuck out of the water. We had come within about 40 feet of it. It didn't take much deduction to realize that we had overshot Miami Beach and were at the south end of Key Biscayne.

We continued north through the rolling troughs and fierce wind and finally arrived at Fort Lauderdale's docks. Wet and exhausted, we cleared customs, had breakfast (those of us who weren't seasick), and motored past Fort Everglades and through the canals to home port. We regretted the 33 hours of sailing missed, and the party dispersed for their various locations.

Night Monsters

When night is deep, monsters creep,
children, men, and women weep.
No one dares to fall asleep.
Monsters creep when night is deep.

When mind fiends fright, peace takes flight.
Nightmares hold us trembling tight
and assault us in the night.
Peace takes flight when mind fiends fright.

When minds can't rest, we protest;
it is a harsh mental test.
And Devil's thoughts do us molest.
We protest when minds can't rest.

We think we'll die, then we cry
when ghosts look us in the eye.
We seek relief from on high,
then we cry, we think we'll die.

Nights that stun are never done,
no place to hide nor to run.
Please God, we yearn for the sun.
Never done are nights that stun.

I had my first real job, and began my career as an Antiquarian Bookseller, at a general bookstore in Boston and was paid seventy-five dollars a week. It was in Boston and I went there on the train from Milton. The Star Book Company and Ernie Star specialized in

American Literature. He had it arranged alphabetically by author and I learned what the rarities of each author were by their absence. Ernie did an interesting thing: he stockpiled American Fiction, 1875 to 1900. When the bibliography, *Wright III*, came out he sold these previously more or less worthless titles to Ohio State and other libraries. On day we went to an auction house in Cambridge which was having a book sale. The sale opened at eight and we got there, along with other dealers and book collectors, at seven. It was January and we were all bitter cold. And I mean really cold. I stayed with Ernie Star for about a year.

From there I went to Harold Burstein in Waltham, just outside of Boston. Harold specialized in Americana, but he dealt in all books. He left me pretty much alone and I catalogued a great variety of items. I remember we went together to Dr. Frederick Meek's house to buy his Henry Wadsworth Longfellow collection. It was a large collection. Harold offered $1,000 for it. Meek talked him up to $15,000! I catalogued it all and we put out a special list devoted to it. Libraries had money then and we got hundreds of numbers, eventually selling most of the collection. Generally, I was cataloguing with a man named Dan Siegel who was a book collector. He was getting paid in rare books.

After about a year with Harold, I went to Harvard to work for Jacob Blanck for the Bibliographical Society of America. While working for Blanck I wrote an analytical essay on William Ellery Channing's popular book *Slavery*, 1835, and an essay on *Early American Signed Cloth Bindings*. Both for the *American Book Collector*. Blanck was one of the first Jews to make a name for himself as a bibliographer, a profession dominated by the WASP elite. We worked in a small room in the Houghton Rare Book Library and I worked on Longfellow for the Bibliography of American Literature. The project eventually grew to seven volumes, and I learned a lot. But eventually I got fired for an excess of enthusiasm. I also asked for more money to go to the University of Virginia to compare notes for the bibliography. At some point I thought I wanted to be an analytical bibliographer which is a person who describes, in minute detail, how books are made and put together. Analytical bibliography has been described as the handmaiden of scholarship and is generally conducted in libraries. So I went to school at night and got a master's degree in Library Science. In fact, I taught the course in bibliography. But I never used it and I went back to work with Harold Burstein.

I then worked for Dan Siegel, cataloguing every kind of book. Dan specialized in American Thought and quirky stuff and I learned a lot there. This lasted for another year, until I moved to New Ipswich, New Hampshire to start my own business. My apprenticeship was over.

When my second son, Mason, came along the Captain Robert Bennet Forbes house was too large, too much of a struggle to get up and down the stairs, so we moved to a small house on another estate in Milton. We played a lot in the fields in which there was high grass and a lot of small holes to hide in. One day I discovered Mason lifting the tail of a cow to see what was there. It was a little dangerous because the cow could have rolled over on him.

During a vacation on the West Coast Mary and the boys and I went to Yosemite and stayed at the famous Ahwahnee in one of their cabins in the woods. We went to dinner and afterward Mary retired early. After a while she came running back from our cabin and said there was a bear in it. Apparently we had left some food in a bag and the bear had come in a window and gone out another window, breaking both screens. We talked to the hotel and they said the bear would probably not come back. But we didn't want to sleep there and insisted they give us a room in the hotel proper. In the morning I walked to the parking lot and saw a car with its front door nearly torn off. I'm sure it was the same bear.

In September the whole world smelled like apples. My wife and I and our young boys lived about a quarter mile from and an apple orchard on the Morrison Farm in Peterborough, New Hampshire about an hour and a half from Boston. The Morrison's hired migrant workers from Mexico to pick the apples. So we went to the orchard after the migrants had left, in the late evening, just before sundown, with our baskets and bags. Some of the apples were on the ground, and had split in half like baked apples—which accounted for the sweet fragrance. There were so many apples that the Morrison's didn't really care if we took some. So my wife and I picked and I lifted the smallest boy up so he could reach and pick too. When we had picked enough we went home with our treasure. We ate some and my wife made apple jelly with the rest. The jelly and the apples were so good.

In the North Part of Vermont

It is cold and I am old
in the north part of Vermont
where people shiver and are gaunt.
At night I hear the crackling of frozen birches
like distant small arms, pistol shots.
And I recall the muffled crunch
of boots on frozen snow.
It is nearly time to go.

From the frosted bedroom window, I see a frigid moon.
The wood-stove fires have gone out
and must be lit again soon.
The pale morning sun will only glimmer next;
gray days are long, with no familiar family song
to help them pass away.
For I am old and I am cold
and not long here to stay.

Alone, I think of other times:
my two young sons in their beds,
now grown and worlds away
in Oregon and Arizona.
And my wife, their mother, warm beside me;
a family together.
Their mother is gone forever now;
I never thought she'd go, never.

We split firewood in the shed,
the boys and I,
and stacked it high
and built snow-forts for fun.
There was talk then and laughter,
and my wife and I were one.
To be all together again
would surly warm the weather.

One winter, in the wood shed,
we found a fox:
Stark, rigid, flat, dry,
dehydrated, dead.
It was thin as sheet metal.
I could have used the fox
by its tail, a stiff handle,
as a snow-shovel.

Sometimes I dream
nectarine dreams of dappled sunbeams
under a coconut palm,
where sailboats swarm and the sea is warm,
and the mind is qualm-less calm.

But I won't go south. I will stay here
and not seek encouragement,
and not find nourishment,
and let the fires go out,
and become shivered and gaunt,
and go the way of the fox.
For it is cold and I am old
In the north part of Vermont.

In New Ipswich we bought an old schoolhouse one half of which
had been converted into living quarters and the other half was a
large open room which needed fixing up. We did fix it up and added
bookcases all around which shelved our books. We stayed there for a
couple of years, and then moved to another house in Peterborough,
added a large wing to accommodate the books and my business took
off. Meanwhile I would get depressed and have to go to a hospital or
see a psychiatrist.

Allan Hardy

O Allan Hardy you sly old country man,
Deep with local knowledge.
I'll plumb your secrets if I can.
You are sinking metal rods into the lawn,
Ten feet apart, attached to extensions cords
trailing from your door.
When you bend what do you put into that coffee can?
I reach you and am shocked to see worms pulsing up from the grass.
No need to dig up the lawn that way.
Two days ago we drank whisky in your cluttered kitchen
After fishing in your hidden lake in the wood.
Now we'll go fishing once more, in the light rain.

The fishing will be good.
Then the warm, coursing whisky again.

We had a family dog, a black Labrador named Friend, for about six years. At a corner of the apple orchard was a stream which formed a small pond and then went under the road. It froze over in the winter. Friend went out on the ice and fell through it. Fortunately, my boys rescued him, otherwise he would have drowned. But Friend began to travel with a bad crowd and one day the farmer shot him for harassing his cows. I swear I heard him scratching at the door for months afterward.

Mary I went to the Eastern Shore of Maryland to buy some books from people who had answered on of our advertisements. The driveway was a mile long and covered with oyster shells. When we got to the house and looked at the library all of the books were in original boards and in very good condition. But the library had been divided by the large family at one time and most of the books were odd volumes. Imagine the novels of James Fennimore Cooper and Charles Dickens and others existing there in only one of their two or three volumes! We were greatly disappointed but bought a few other books. Then I noticed that Robert E. Lee had carved his initials in one of the old window panes. Evidently he had courted one of the daughters. There was also an original Rembrandt Peale painting: a family portrait! Later on, back in Boston, we were browsing through a book of historic American homes and realized we had been in one on the Eastern Shore of Maryland.

I got interested in parrots and had a Golden-crowned Conure for a while. But I smoked, not knowing that cigarette smoke is toxic to birds. He lived in a bathroom and died one day. I buried him along the Esplanade next to the Charles River.

My sons are good men: they don't smoke, drink or do drugs and never have. But one week we called the week from hell. Stephen had worked summers for College Pro Painters. He was a manager and did very well. The next summer he decided to do his own business and went to Nantucket. He was pleased with himself and bragged a little. College Pro got wind of it and decided to sue him for doing business within twenty-five miles of their own and for using College Pro's painting manuals. So he called from Nantucket and asked me to get him a lawyer. I called John Wallace, now a lawyer in Atlanta, who gave me an attorney from Hale & Dorr in Boston. I told Steve he would have to pay for the lawyer himself. Steve came home and went to court on Monday. It was a nonsense suit. When they got to court and the Hale & Dorr man yelled out "have you seen a lawyer around here in a seersucker suit?" The College Pro man disappeared in a hurry so the suit never came to trial.

In the meantime, Mason, who was supposedly helping Steve in Nantucket, came back to Boston. He was going to a very good school, the Commonwealth School, and had janitorial responsibilities and a key to get in. He went inside the school with his girlfriend and spent the night. In the morning they were caught climbing out a window. So they both went to jail and then to court. Mason was embarrassed and wouldn't tell us about his escapade so a friend of his phoned us and told us. Mason thought he could talk his way out of it. But of course he couldn't. The girl was let loose to go home. And Mason went off to college at the University of Pennsylvania on probation. So ended the week from hell.

Mary was a big asset in our business. She developed our appraisal business and appraised all the manuscripts. We appraised the Salem Athenaeum, the Kress Collection at Harvard Business School, a collection of 16th and 17th British plays in Cleveland, Ohio, the property of a man who had frozen to death at Gettysburg during a reenactment of the battle, the library of Henry Ford III, and various others. At that time Lou Lehrman and Richard Gilder were buying American manuscripts relating to the Revolutionary War and the Civil War hand over fist and Mary appraised all these as gifts to the Pierpont Morgan Library several years after they bought them.

The University of Florida had purchased an outstanding collection of American literature and we, and other distinguished bibliographers, went there to write the analytical bibliographies of the authors. Mary and I worked on Henry Wadsworth Longfellow. I got very depressed so much of the credit for the work belongs to Mary.

I have always been interested in sailing and sailed in Boston Bay with my friend Bob Brennen. We also participated in some small races and went out to the islands. We took a trip once and sailed up to New Hampshire. On the way back the fog was so thick that we arrived in home port seven hours, at night, later than we should have. It was a scary business. I also took a course in sailing in Florida for my birth day. I also went to Marathon, Florida for my fortieth birthday to get my sailing certifications. And I did, obtaining Coastal Cruising in two weeks. While there we went further south to Key West and saw the schooner Olad from Camden, Maine which wintered in Florida. The instructor thought I was a good sailor and wanted to know if I would help take someone's boat up the waterway to Norfolk, but I declined.

I Have Stood Trembling

before the Devil, and looked into his
evil, sulphurous
eyes.
I have felt his awful magnetism,
been shrouded in his darkest cloak of pain,
suffocated in his putrid bog of mental fog.
I have survived his worst temptations:
his bridges
his guns

his pills
his ropes
his shrieking fucking madnesses.
I walk unsteadily now—from the stinking nearness of It.
I've sworn he won't enslave my mind again,
and I know the Devil lies.
Yet I wake each day with wary, watchful eyes
because I know, too, that the Devil never dies.

The Pit

I never wanted to believe the signs: a vague nervousness, a rapidly decreasing tolerance for frustration which manifested as small temper tantrums, and a tendency to startle easily as if some shadowy thing or person were following me. A sharp sound, a shadow on The wall at night, The clicking shoes of a person passing from behind, The telephone ringing, an agoraphobic dizziness when shopping in malls—any of These things might jangle my increasingly hypersensitive nerves. These were physical sensations not of fear exactly but startle reflexes accompanied by an erratic strumming of my heart: precursors of my mind going wrong. I became manic too: a rapid flow of ideas, a pressure to speak, an unaccustomed euphoric optimism, a tendency to try to fit too much into the day, sleepless nights.

Then my mood would change and the descent into darkness and the onslaught of mental pain would begin. I would deride myself for not being a better person. Obsession with real or imagined faults would plague me like warts on the brain. Hordes of unpleasant thoughts crowded my mind like maggots: my imagined lack of material success, my regret over trivial sins of omission and commission, the feeling that I was simply no good. I ruminated on my occasional careless behavior toward family and friends, most of it ancient and trivial. I paced the apartment and checked again and again that the doors and windows were locked. I chain-smoked and drank cup after cup of coffee. I called a few friends but hung up when they answered. I couldn't work, concentrate, or read; my sad, tortured representative thoughts became a dismal fugue. I tried desperately to get control of my runaway mind but could not.

Then my body went awry: my eyelids twitched, my ears rang or droned on; I spoke slowly and in halting unfinished sentences; I couldn't remember where I'd put things; I developed aches and pains with no discernible cause; and, as my mind slowed, I could hardly keep awake. I stayed in The apartment and closed out the world. The pills I had taken for years became useless. I drank too much. I used alcohol to self-medicate, to find solace, to forget, to alleviate the pain, and to sleep at night. Wrapped in a shroud of misery created by my own self-abusive thoughts, I sweated and ran hot and cold. I stayed in bed day and night, sleeping or tossing, haunted by my inadequacies. The simplest tasks took monumental effort which I abandoned as the endless days passed. I didn't shave, I didn't brush my teeth, I didn't shower, my breath was feted, my eyes dull, my breathing labored. I took pleasure in nothing. All this feasted on my feasted on my mental health and mired me in an obsessive mental fog from which there was no escape. I became trapped, as if in a cesspool with toxic waste rising to engulf me, or as if my body and mind were fatally bogged in quicksand.

The final defeat, which came on gradually, was when I could no longer chew or swallow solid food. At first I ate very slowly, chewing with effort and trying hard to ignore what was happening. Eventually, and it always brought me to tears, I could not eat normal meals and was reduced to drinking for fortified fruit juices, yogurt and liquid weight-gain concoctions. At this stage, I was devastated by the knowledge that I had completely lost control of myself and was reduced to a child-like state. I had lost my will and my personality; my ego had disintegrated. I was terribly unwell: the blackness was thick, the mental pain agonizing, the misery complete, the depression unrelenting, and my terror of life and preoccupation with death were unquenchable. I had lost my sanity. So I tried to die.

I was bi-polar and suffered ravaging depressions every several years. I was a fifty-year old book dealer who did business from my large Boston apartment David L O'Neal Antiquarian Bookseller. My wife could do nothing about it except cover for me when I was in the hospital. I issued catalogues of old and rare books and sent Them to collectors, libraries, museums, and other dealers. And I was a reasonable success in a difficult profession. Fortunately, although I didn't think it was fortunate after I woke up in The hospital my home Mary had come in on a hunch and, finding me unconscious on the floor, had dialed 911.

I woke up in The Intensive Care Unit of Massachusetts General Hospital. Dazed and confused, I had an IV line in my wrist, a sore throat, an upset stomach from the charcoal administered to absorb the toxicity of the pills I'd overdosed with, and a dull but persistent taste in my mouth. I had lost thirty-five pounds and was thin and wretched. But, while plenty sick, my mood had peaked and The crisis was over. Two days later an ambulance took me to the maximum security ward of The Arbor Hospital, a short-term crisis center for The mentally ill.

My first major depression had struck in my early twenties. I had stayed in each of these hospitals for about three months. The Arbor, so named for a puny trellis on the grounds with a few scraggly grape vines clinging to it, was a lowly, tough place. It was the pits.

The "Pit" was twenty-five feet square, three sides being formed by The hospital walls, the fourth by a single twelve-foot high concrete wall. It was entered through a thick glass door in one of the hospital walls. The Pit was where The inmates smoked six or eight times a day, usually by a rigorous schedule, while The psych nurses stayed in The hallway and kept an eye on Their charges. The patients mostly ignored the several black plastic ashtrays scattered on the concrete floor of the Pit so that The ground was often a mess of fag ends, candy wrappers and other debris. The Pit, rarely cleaned, was raw, especially when it rained and smelled even more of tobacco, spit, and urine and, sometimes, vomit.

For those patients who didn't have cigarettes, there were "community cigarettes" which were donated by The staff or by The better off inmates who had brought their own. You could also give money to a selected nurse who would buy them for you on their way home. The majority of the patients, many of whom were addicted to drugs or alcohol, smoked. Some of those that didn't would go to The Pit anyway for a change of venue and for outside air. There was an aura of menace in The Pit and usually one ward at a time was taken there. If two wards were in The Pit at The same time the possibility of mischief was greater.

I always kept a sharpened pencil in my pocket when I was in the Pit. I kept my hand on it and would often push it outward so that it was clear to others. There were at least to those few who were in good enough shape to notice, that I was carrying a potential weapon. It was small comfort. I had been to The Arbor hospital three previous times and each time, when I was up to it, I intentionally made friends with one of The biggest men there, crazy or not. And I would hang out in The Pit with my friend. It was safer that way. My current inside friend and Pit buddy, Jack, was a big wacko man who liked to talk, guiltily, about my misbehaviors, including sodomizing a cow.

I recovered slowly in my single room and shared bathroom at The Arbor. The last time I was There I was given shock treatment, The euphemism for which was Electro Convulsive Therapy. I had it three times. Meals were served at 7:00, 12:00 and 6:00, and I ate them. Meds were given out before bed time, and I took them. There were hour-long "groups" throughout the day, which at first I was too tired or depressed to attend: art and music therapy, medical education, nutrition, cognitive behavioral therapy, and so forth. These were low-level classes and boring, but after a few days I went to most of them because I knew cooperation was part of the process that would lead to my release. I knew my recovery was a waiting game: eventually the depression would burn itself out and I would return to normal functioning. It was always that way. But, in the meantime, aside from television at night (ironically ER was a favorite on the ward). The routine was stultifying and for a while there were no doctors. Later, when I had sufficiently recovered my sanity, I would see the hospital psychiatrist assigned to me twice a week. At first I kept to myself, sleeping or dozing; then I slowly began to interact with the other patients, that is with those who were approachable. Some of the permanently mad and other poor souls on the ward would be transferred to longer-term hospitals: the schizophrenics, psychotics, paranoids, and psychopaths. Many took fistfuls of different medicine, others were depressed or manic and, like me, had attempted suicide; some were drug addicts or alcoholics, prostitutes, homeless, or criminals such as Miles O'Connor, son of a policeman, who reputedly masterminded the theft of The Rembrandts and other paintings from The Gardener Museum in Boston. These would be released in due course; many would return to The Arbor again and again. Some would be remanded to homeless shelters or half-way houses or longer term rehabilitation programs courtesy of the state or of the federal government. A number were Vietnam veterans. A few faces were vaguely familiar to me from previous stays.

Many of the psych nurses, men and women, were Haitians and I knew some of them. Some were friendly and helpful; some were lazy and begrudging; a few were tyrants relishing their power over the insane and the down and out. The nurses were important to an inmate because they could get you things: pencil and paper, a board game or playing cards, change for the telephone or for the candy machines. And they could ask the doctors to see you sooner rather than later or relay questions to the doctors, and so forth. These little favors made life inside easier and they were unique opportunities. I made friends with the nurses by speaking French to them. Most of them responded favorably to my efforts and treated reasonably nicely.

I played the game well and practicing my French was the only real pleasure I had at the Arbor.

I was scared that I would be stuck at The Arbor, although it could never happen because the hospital didn't want patients to stay very long—once their crises were over and they were considered no longer a danger to themselves or to others they were released. And I was terrified of not be able to use the telephone. Phoning was not easy: local calls required the right change; long distance calls were almost impossible, so I always kept a paid-up telephone card or two in my wallet. Of course wallet, keys, belt, shoelaces, and even dental floss were taken from me upon admittance. But they did give I back my telephone cards. I could never figure out how a patient could do himself harm with dental floss, but I was told by a nurse that people could be very creative. Nobody came to see me; I didn't want company at The Arbor; the phone was my lifeline to the outside world.

One of the patients at The Arbor in the maximum security ward was a street punk, a tough obnoxious nineteen-year old who gave the nurses a hard time. He was thin and wiry, spoke in hate-jive, wouldn't take my medicine, and was often out of control. An older tattooed weight-lifter, put him down and threatened worse if the punk didn't behave. For a while he calmed down and stopped threatening everyone, but then the nurses had to hold him down, give him I an injection of Thorazine, and put him into the "quiet room" until he emerged with a different attitude.

There were four wards at The Arbor: A: The maximum security ward where every admitted patient was first taken to and vetted; B, a somewhat more relaxed ward for the emotionally ill; C, a ward for drug addicts and alcoholics; and D, the locked but least secure ward for patients who were better and on their way out. After three and a half weeks I was transferred to D Ward and to my surprise I found a woman there I knew from the outside. Jennifer told me she was at The Arbor because she had been mentally abused by her husband, and

I recalled that her mental health had always been fragile. I consoled her as much as possible.

In D Ward, patients were escorted for walks at least once a day if they wanted to go out. Accompanied by a nurse, they would walk together around the small grounds on which The Arbor was situated, always for some reason from right to left around the property. Sometimes they would sit for a smoke and chat with each other or with the nurse, or pass a football around. As most of the patients had been legally committed to The Arbor, they could not just leave when they wanted to. So these walks created opportunities for escape, although in my previous two stays at The Arbor I had not attempted to do so.

I had been in The Arbor slightly over five weeks. I was bored and impatient and wanted out. I'd never heard of anyone leaving before their time. But I was ready. One day on a walk, I drifted to the end of the line of about eight strung out patients and when they had turned a corner, having some change in my pocket for bus fare, I just scooted off. Nervously, but elated with my freedom, I trotted down the road to Main Street and caught the number 38 bus to Copley Square which was near my Back Bay apartment. The apartment was on the ground floor of a large Beacon Street building and my living room windows faced the Charles River. A hidden key to the apartment was sunk into the soil of an outside planter on one of the windows sills.

I knew that, notified by the hospital of my leave-taking, the police would come. They police came at about 4:00 pm; I was ready for them and persuaded them that I was all right and needn't go back to the hospital. At 4:45 my doctor from the hospital called. I told the psychiatrist that I was okay now which was apparently, I thought, just what the doctor wanted to hear. The hospital didn't like the way I left but didn't really want me back; there were new patients and failed suicides the Arbor needed to make room for.

Slowly I settled into my normal routine. Then and eventually became completely myself again, which was always the case. I talked to my psychiatrist at Harvard Pilgrim, my HMO. I opened the mail, processed some orders, played tennis with a friend, researched some books I had acquired, and began to put together a new catalogue. I saw a few friends. Then I settled down to the usual work week.

I wondered where these depressions came from. Certainly, as the transformation from health to illness took place, there were chemical changes in my brain, imbalances of neuro-chemicals, that much was plain. When I was in the depths of it, my brain and body were radically changed, proof of the strong mind-body connection. But what set my depressions off? What were the triggers? Why did they occur every three or four years with perfectly normal good periods in between? I sensed that if I could figure out their cause or causes, I could modify my behavior, cut the depressions off at the pass, and avoid the devastation. But they were mysterious, causeless events to both me and my doctors. Did they happen at a particular time of year? I didn't think so. There was no apparent seasonal pattern. Was there a purpose to these nightmarish episodes? Surly not to punish me, unless I was subconsciously punishing myself. Over the years various anti-depressant and mood-stabilizes had been tried. Did they work? I didn't know if they worked or not but didn't dare find out by not taking them. And I had seen psychotherapist off and on to no apparent avail. Most of the time, after I had recovered, I put it all behind me. What could I do but soldier on? But the shadow was always there: my deeper self, my unconscious, my devils. I was my own nemesis, and I could never predict when the evil would strike again.

The oddest thing was that, after a while, I realized that, although I would never admit it to anyone and just barely to myself, I missed the hospitals, I even missed The Arbor and The Pit. I missed the meals prepare for me, I missed speaking French, I missed the drama of patients getting into it with each other, I missed the perceived danger, I missed some of the nurses. But most of all, although I certainly didn't want to go back there, I missed the down time. I missed getting out of the day to day firing line, I missed avoiding the press of business, and I mostly missed—what was it exactly that I particularly missed? Shamefully I thought that I mostly missed being taken care of once in a while when life got too much for me. It was a dangerous, screwed up psychology. Because, deep down inside, I knew I'd be back at the Arbor or similar place one of these years, even though I might have to try to kill myself trying not to go there.

I drove seventy thousand miles a year for several years seeking rare books. And I depended somewhat on my Harvard friends buying catalogues for reference purposes, individual rare books, and several interesting collections. I bought a collection of duplicate type specimens from the David Wheatland collection one time and early scientific books and classics another time. These books were in Latin, Greek, French and Italian. I continued to check with Harvard for duplicates but became less dependent upon them as time went by. One time I got fixated on a famous book, the *Nuremberg Chronicle*, 1493, an illustrated history of the world printed in 1493. I figured every bookseller should have one and it was an extremely difficult book to sell. It was difficult for about ten years or so but eventually got easier as sellers began to come to us.

We lived in New Hampshire for fifteen years and then moved to Boston, renting at first and doing business from home, then living in a friend's house on Beacon Hill, and then we bought a very nice condo on Beacon Street and doing business from an office on Dartmouth Street.

It was a manic-depressive business because I would get so depressed that I couldn't work or drive anywhere looking for books. So I would stay in bed for a couple of weeks, then I'd feel better and go charging around. Down and out, then up and about, down and out, then up and about! One time I got so depressed that I headed for New Hampshire to buy a gun and surly would have shot myself. But the

Massachusetts police required a permit so I didn't get the gun. Several times Mary found me passed out on the floor when I had overdosed.

Mary and I and my oldest son, Steve, went to Japan to go to Mason's wedding. The bride and groom were all dressed up in traditional Japanese clothes and looked charming. After the wedding we went to Mt Fujiyama and stayed at a Japanese hotel.

It was a beautiful, warm evening and I was in a great mood because of a successful business conference in the South End of Boston. I was walking down Marlboro Street, that narrow, shady street, where I lived, when a black man approached me. He was young, about my height (six feet), dressed nicely but casually, and started to tell me a story. Speaking without accent and he told me he lived in Worcester, Mass. (about 75 miles down the turnpike) and that he had parked his car by accident along the side of the road in a no parking area between the Boston Common and the Boston Garden. The car, a two years old Honda, had been towed away. He only had Thirty dollars and needed another thirty to pay the fine to get it back. He said he worked for a meat packer down by Boston Harbor and gave me that phone number as well as his number and address in Worcester. He seemed nice young man in distress.

So I gave him the thirty dollars. Then he told me he needed a little more to get a taxi to the garage where his car was. But I didn't have any more. So I said "Well let's go to my local ATM on Newberry Street." And he said, out of the blue, "You're not afraid of me, are you." And I replied "No, should I be?"

So we sauntered over across Commonwealth Avenue to the ATM which was like a closet, a covered area and there was already somebody there. When she left, I withdrew about twenty dollars and gave it to him. We said goodbye to each other and I wished him luck.

The next day, growing somewhat apprehensive about being paid back, I called the Worcester number and of course it was the wrong number. Then I phoned the number of the meat packer he'd given me. There was no such business at that number. Of course I had been skunked.

About a week later, I met another black man, in more or less the same place. When he asked me for money because his car was towed away, I told him I'd already been victimized by that scam and started yelling at him as he rapidly disappeared down the street. So much for generosity!

Commonwealth Avenue Fugue

In winter,
when we go to Aspen,
they hang out in the doorways of office buildings
or by the warm exhaust vents
on Blagdon Street behind the Public Library.
No fugue in the cold.
But in summer...

8:00 am:

Three strident voices
from Public Alley 432
boom up the back stairwell
of my fine Commonwealth Avenue apartment
and resonate through the pantry and kitchen
to the dining room,
where I have breakfast
of poached eggs, kippered herring,
ice-cold grapefruit juice,
and Oolong tea from Taiwan.

Fortissimo words with
clanking of garbage can lids,
bouncing of bottles,
shattering of glass or china,
dropping and plopping of paper bags.
Loud, loud words of the temporarily sober
turned out of the shelter early,
according to the rules,
and unable to return before 4:00 pm.
Sometimes these haggard homeless find
useful items in the refuse: edible food,
sweater, shirt, pants, an old coat for winter.
Now and then they fight with words,
but occasionally they poke and push each other
further scattering and rattling the cans.

10:30 am:

Now this raucous off-key trio
in dirty jeans and t-shirts
bench themselves in the shade of Commonwealth Avenue trees
swigging cheap wine,
sharing cigarettes lip to hand to lip and
speaking in short phrases
punctuated by mild obscenities
while passersby in suits and dresses ignore them.
Or they whistle at women.
Through the elegant bay window of my parlor
I watch these harmless hairy men become besotted.
As I stroll past them
on the way to my club for a lunch
of romaine salad and deviled eggs,
they seldom panhandle;

but if they ask I say "Not this time."
The tall one wearing my old blue dress shirt,
French cuffs rolled up, once said
"Aw, you always say that, man. How about some flowers?"
As time passes, they drink to a noisy crescendo
then taper off, adagio,
to a mumbled finale, then silence.

2:30 pm:

Passed out on the benches or ground,
they sleep in the sun
then totter up to the Boston Garden or Common
and congregate with their kind
around the T-station entrances
or near the public restrooms of the Tourist Information Building
where there stay until
back to the shelter for dinner.

Next morning:
the same men,
the same dissonant music in the alley.

The Beast

Midway along my path of life
an horrid beast blocked the way
And I was stunned with sudden strife.

"Turn back," the beast seemed to say.
With blood-stained claws and fiery cast,
The beast was fearsome in every way.

It would not move, nor let me past
So my fear dragged on and on
Until I fainted and fell, aghast.

When I woke up the beast was gone
And I was all alone again
Knowing I must get up and go on.

I'd known this beast before, but when?
What could this awful creature be?
This vile deformed energumen.

And as I walked, I understood then
That the snarling beast had been me
And I felt crappy.

We closed the business down in 2002 and I came to the San Francisco Bay area, where both my sons and grandchildren now live. At first I lived alone on a houseboat in Sausalito then I moved into San Francisco proper and bought a house right across from the Rose Garden in Golden Gate Park.

AA

When my marriage of many years, which ended in divorce, was unraveling, I drank every night and made the drinks stronger and stronger. Sometimes I would stop off at a bar on the way home and now and then I would skip dinner. Of course this behavior distressed my then wife and made the prospect of saving our marriage less and less likely. Being a member of the "cocktail generation" and at that time in my mid-fifties, I had indulged in a drink or two every night for a very long time. I began to wonder if I could stop if I wanted to; I began to wonder if I was an alcoholic.

So I started going to Alcoholics Anonymous in Boston and continued to do so for several years. Because I worked for and by myself, and because I am bi-polar and subject to depression, I did not have a large network of friends and was not particularly at ease in social situations. In addition to making some good friends in AA, while I never stopped drinking entirely, the experience of AA allowed me to radically change my drinking habits. I discovered that I was not an alcoholic and that I didn't have to drink every night. It was powerful self-knowledge to know that I could take it or leave it.

And there was another, equally useful, benefit from AA. As a child, I had a severe stuttering problem which sometimes rendered me mute. The stutter had to do, almost certainly, with my father who was a distant, taciturn, intimidating man who seldom talked to me and, when on rare occasions he did, he turned away with impatience at my hesitant speech. My stuttering continued through grammar school, high school, and college where I avoided asking questions in class or participating in any activity such as discussion groups, student councils, or dramatic productions. The stutter persisted through a brief military service and for a good part of my adult working life. I spoke mostly in one-liners, avoided telling long stories, and preferred to communicate by letter rather than by telephone. I am still occasionally bothered by stuttering, but the problem is much diminished.

In my profession as an Antiquarian Bookseller I garnered a fair amount of arcane specialized knowledge and, over the years, was asked to speak before book-bibliophile clubs and rare book libraries. But I was terrified of public speaking and always turned down these invitations. Knowing, however, that such talks would be good for my career, and because I felt cowardly not stepping up to the podium (so to speak), turning down these speaking engagements always made me feel bad about myself. It was, here, in addition to changing my drinking pattern, that AA was also a great help.

AA meetings have various formats: some are small groups of people who sit around a table and discuss abstract concepts as honesty, persistence, and love; others are large groups that have different primary speakers at each meeting; still others create opportunities for anyone to speak about some aspect of the twelve steps. The atmosphere and environment in all formats is trusting, secure, encouraging, and supportive. In most any type of meeting there is the opportunity, indeed sometimes the requirement, to speak up before the group. To a large extent, AA is about overcoming fear (especially the fear of having to deal with life sober); over time in this therapeutic community I became more and more comfortable speaking before groups. So much so that one day, when the Director of the Boston Athenaeum Library asked me to speak to its members on some aspect of rare books, I said yes, albeit with trepidation.

During the next several weeks, I worked on my talk about fore-edge paintings. Fore-edge paintings, which flourished in the 19th century, are watercolor pictures, usually landscapes, painted on the oblique edges of leather bound books and then concealed beneath gold so the images can be seen only when the pages of the books so decorated are fanned. I was terrified about the upcoming event and practiced endlessly with the curator of rare books at the Athenaeum—a friend who would show slides as I referred to various examples. I was stricken with anxiety that I would not be able to pull off the talk. I slept fitfully, mumbled sentences and paragraphs of the talk all the time, and became thoroughly obsessed and stressed with the whole idea of speaking effectively to a large group of strangers. My slide-presenter grew impatient with me and thought I was nuts. Even though I got to know the material perfectly, I was fearful of failure. Several days before the event I had an inspired idea: I asked three of my AA friends to come to the lecture and to "Please sit in the front row." Sensitive persons that they were, they understood immediately why I wanted them there.

Much to my relief, subsequent joy, and everlasting thanks to a "higher power," the talk was a success. During the rest of my working life, I gave two other talks. Then I decided not to do them anymore, although I knew I could. I made a rational decision that was no longer driven by fear. To a large extent, the ability to make such a decision was a result of my experience of and participation in AA. For which, to this day, I am grateful.

And by the way, I met Elton John at an AA meeting in the downtown post office.

In 2002 Mary and I were divorced. In part because I had cheated on her and in part because she thought she could now make it on her own as an appraiser. It was a relatively easy divorce and we split our finances down the middle.

I walked down the corridors of the San Francisco Airport with Streak, my parrot, on my shoulder and was met by my oldest son and we then headed for the houseboats.

Streak and I had many adventures and now I want t tell you one: Streak was startled by loud noises and one morning about 9:00, when I was refueling at the local Shell station, a car behind us honked. Streak flew off precipitously at the loud noise and flew up into one of the tall trees which was a short way off. For the next eight hours, continually apprehensive that a hawk would get her, I tried everything to get Streak to come down: throwing rocks and branches, climbing the tree to offer Streak a stick for a perch to descent upon (I couldn't get high enough), and asking a couple of young gas station attendants to climb even higher. When they couldn't get high enough I called the fire department but their ladders could find no purchase on the tree. During this time it was evident, from the fluttering of her wings, that Streak wanted to come down, but she couldn't quite do it or couldn't decide to do it. At 5:00 PM that afternoon I drove home to the houseboat to get Streak some bird food and her cage. Then I drove back to where the trees were and parked the car under them with the cage open in the hatchback.

I was tired and despairing by sundown and could no longer see my parrot so I left for home to get some sleep—all the while hoping that Streak would have the good sense to fly down to her cage during the night. After a fretful and fitful night at 5:30 the next morning I walked back to the car. No Streak, nor could I see her. I shuffled back home, dejected. At 9:30 I went back to the tree and with difficulty I spotted Streak high in the branches. We whistled back and forth for a while, then I climbed the tree again and got close enough to her to fling a dead branch her way. The branch caused her to off across the highway to a smaller tree, bu after two hours trying to get her down, I tweaked her with a long wooden rod obtained from the car wash. This simply caused her to fly east over several warehouses and disappear out of sight. I drove up and down several streets where I thought she might be and called to her to no avail. Then I went for breakfast at a nearby café. I was so worried that I had lost Streak forever that I had difficulty eating. Just as I was about to give up, I heard my parrot's beseeching cry from an unclear direction. Eventually I pinpointed the sound and found her in a tree whose top rose above the flat roof of a warehouse. I climbed the roof, leaned out to the tree, and offered her my arm. She took it. The next day I had her wings clipped!

The Castro

On a warm Saturday afternoon
in the parish of the Most Holy Redeemer Catholic Church
under the Rainbow flag at busy Harvey Milk Plaza,
corner Castro and Market Streets,

tables and chairs are set out in the sun
where gay men in shorts and tank-tops,
or bare-chested in tight jeans,
display their gym-buffed bodies.
Some are embracing or kissing,
most are cruising: waiting, watching, wanting.

Buck Naked and the Bare Bottom Boys
used to play their rendition of
"Bend Over Baby and Let Me Drive"
at the annual Castro Street Fair or on Gay Pride Day.
And there's still plenty of naked:
two middle-aged bare-assed men,
one black, one white,
sit quietly in the Plaza for an hour,
after which they saunter south down Castro Street
calm and composed, dicks and balls gently swinging
while gaping tourists take pictures.
The two nude men stop at a billboard pasted with notices for
Queer Print Making Class, Hella Gay Comedy Show,
Peaches Christ, the Sisters of Perpetual Indulgence,
Locker Room Blow Off,
and other opportunities and sextravaganzas.
Then, ambling past the glorious 1920s Castro Theatre,
with its art-deco interior and multi-cultural architectural features,
the naked men cross 18th Street,
glance at the Free Rapid HIV Testing sign
(call 415-689-MASH—Mobile Allies for Sexual Health)
above the Bank of America
and peer into the joint offices
of the LGBTQ community's Human Rights Campaign
and Trevor Project for crisis intervention
and suicide prevention.

Further on, these starkers showmen
cross Castro at 19th Street and stroll back north.
Just beyond A. G. Ferrari Foods
they look into a drag costume boutique
("find your inner diva")
and shops such as Auto Erotica,
Does Your Mother Know, and Rock Hard,
which offer Anal Ring Toss, Drill Sergeant,
a Cyber Skin Vibrating Ass, and other such.
Then they sashay past massage parlors and bars including
the already overflowing 440 Castro
with its $2 beer, Weekend Warm Up (Fridays)
Underwear Night (Mondays),
CDXL Outlaw Party for Guys (Thursdays),
and DJ Jim's Go-Go Boys (Wednesdays).
Near the Wells Fargo Bank
the naked men disappear down an alley
leaving a crowd of curious tourists,
neo-punks and funky drifters from Haight-Ashbury,
straight couples from the neighborhood,
lesbians and gays of all ages,
and a dumbstruck poet.

Seeded with thousands of gay servicemen
Off-loaded in San Francisco by the military
during WW II for being homosexual,
the vibrant Castro
with talented artists, writers, and musicians,
is the largest gay neighborhood in the world.

But why such clamor and noisy "in your face?"
There have been gays for two million years—
ever since the birth of Homo Erectus.

The Houseboats of Sausalito

Living on a houseboat is cool. Not cool as in "not as warm as Florida," but cool like Andy Garcia, the Toyota Prius hybrid, mango ice-cream, and Independent voters. I moved to Sausalito recently from the East Coast and intend to stay here because the nature of the Bay Area is so startlingly diverse and beautiful. And I live on a floating home, to boot.

I treasure the houseboats because they are special: the men here don't wear ties and the women don't sport skirts or high-heeled shoes. The only tie I've ever seen was in a box of clothes at the land end of the dock where residents put unwanted items which their neighbors can then poke through and re-cycle if fitting. The only skirts and high-heeled shoes I've seen were in a woman's car, perhaps for a surreptitious night out. And I like the houseboats for the same reasons their owners do: it is quiet and peaceful here, a place to chill out, to heal from whatever ails you (real or imaginary), a safe-haven of refuge and a place to repair from the stress of modern life. Being on and in the water is soothing balm for the soul. And the gentle bobbing, rocking, rising and falling of the homes is perfect for sleeping, day or night.

The sky is bigger here too and the stars brighter than elsewhere. For scenery there are views of Mt. Tam, the Marin Headlands, Angel and Alcatraz Islands, and the San Francisco skyline. And the weather is great. I have walked to the end of my dock in warm, bright sunlight and looked toward San Francisco shrouded in fog. In the evening I watch fog swell and roll over the Marin headlands and come to a stop a half-mile from shore. And there it remains, rarely getting to Richardson Bay and the houseboat marinas.

Dwellers of the floating homes (houseboats which have no means of locomotion) are quirky in the friendliest way. Eccentrics and free-spirited individuals live here, centered to be sure but also slightly out of kilter. Many are at least half way out of the mundane box and are traveling roads less taken. Since their homes are close together, house boaters are helpful to their neighbors in time of need as well as respectful of each other's privacy. Many of my neighbors have some former or present connection to the sea: active or retired navy or coast-guard, shipbuilders, yacht surveyors, marine biologists and ecologists, inveterate sailors, workers at such sea-worthy organizations as the Bay Model. Doctors and lawyers live here too, but no beggar-men or thieves. And I've not seen hermits. Yet that could simply mean they are adept at their minimalist way of living. And it is no surprise that there is a lot of creative talent on these docks: artists, writers, photographers, craftsmen, performers.

My parrot also likes it here. Her wings are not clipped and occasionally she escapes into joyous flight and perches on nearby rooftops. It's a fairly safe environment for her because there is nowhere else for her to fly to except to another houseboat. We are good friends, my parrot and I, but she regards me with aloof disdain when I summon her back home. My neighbors are tolerant when, embarrassed, I knock on their doors and ask permission to get onto their roofs to retrieve the wayward bird. My parrot is the eccentric one in the family, of course, not I.

All houseboats have watercraft of some kind tethered behind them and their owners avail themselves of this most ancient and honorable art of locomotion: canoes, kayaks, rafts, zodiacs, platforms propelled by water-wheels, rowboats, motorboats, and sailboats are everywhere. I go kayaking with my bird on my shoulder. She holds tight to the folds of my shirt and, head cocked to one side, peers into the water as if trying to see her reflection or fathom a mystery. Every morning I see a single scull moving swiftly across the bay and am reminded of Thomas Eakins' famous paintings of rowing on the Schuylkill. Throughout the year, at springtide when the moon is new or full, there are unusually high tides and some of the parking lots flood. At such times residents don their wading boots, negotiate the water in shopping carts, give piggy-back rides to each other, or hold kayak races in the parking lots in several feet of water.

Life on a houseboat tends to be quiet, peaceful, relaxing, fun, and very seductive. Many who move here soon find ways to work from home. There is a serene beauty to living on the water in close harmony with the broad variety of wildlife which surrounds the homes. Birds fly, swim and dive among our homes; we share the environment with an abundance of fascinating creatures. One evening, while sitting with a friend on her back deck, we were joined by neighborhood ducks which waddled up the floating fowl ramps my friend had built for them.

Water acts as a great social leveler; it is impossible not to know those who live on the same dock as I. There is only one way out and one way in and we pass each other frequently. Certain universal houseboat values are apparently shared by everyone: an abiding love of water, an attraction to the ever changing scenery, the sense of community and cooperation. During storms people watch out for their neighbors' houseboats which are, at such times, vulnerable to slipping or breaking their moorings. And when owners rent their homes, a neighbor volunteers to be a sort of superintendent for the temporary resident, overseeing and giving advice and counsel. There is a feeling that we all share the same habitat and the closer we are to our environment, and to each other, the better off we will be. Houseboats occupy the space between solid ground (for solid citizens) and the mythic sea (mermaids, pirates, mysterious creatures), and they share the luxuries of water and sky which impart a sense of plenty. Now and then nearly spontaneous parties erupt on the docks: someone sets out a table and residents show up for conversation with wine and cheese, sausages, dip, cookies and other goodies.

My son, an overworked entrepreneur, visits to watch Sixty Minutes most Sundays. He loves it here and decompresses immediately, slowing down and breathing deeply as soon as his feet hit the dock in a sort of walking meditation. He spends the night and we have an early breakfast outside on the deck. Then he goes back to work refreshed.

I hear the scratchy, clacking sound of seagulls walking on my roof. Sometimes, from a height, they drop muscles onto the roof in order to crack them open. It is like magic here. Small things seem portentous: a circling pelican, a majestic Great Blue Heron tip-toeing thru shallow water, a lone duck, a boat passing closely in the dark. During the day there are constant bird calls, cries and songs, forming a background noise to which I am accustomed and which I welcome. At night it is quiet.

Wildlife is ubiquitous in Richardson Bay. There are crabs, snails, muscles, sea squirts and numerous other invertebrates, as well as pods of seals and the occasional sea lion. Sometimes at night raccoons forage surreptitiously on the docks for cat food and other forbidden nourishment. Harbor seals haul out in the evening onto floating platforms near the houseboats and the territorial males grunt and groan. Among the fish are plainfin midshipman (Porichthys notates,) or Humming Toadfish. Toadfish are nocturnal bottom dwellers and live much of the year off the coast at depths approaching 1,000 feet, feeding mostly on shrimp and burying themselves in sand and mud during the day. In July and August (their mating season) Toadfish move into bays and estuaries and often set up housekeeping underneath the hulls of houseboats. The mating call of the male is a humming or droning sound, a perfect A flat. They hum by vibrating the extraordinarily strong muscles above their swim bladders. These muscles vibrate 6,000 times a minute, twice the speed of the wings of hummingbirds. Toadfish can hum for hours at a time and their "love-songs" will set off the motor-boat like noise of neighboring Toadfish, keeping some house boaters awake all night.

But mostly there are birds. Birds everywhere all the time. Among the shorebirds are time-steps of sandpipers (Least and Western), snowy egrets which, at low tide, step gingerly on spindly legs on the mud flats or in shallow pools, herons (including Great Blue Herons and Black-crowned Night Herons), avocets, clapper rails, widgeons, and ducks. I feed the more or less same paddling of ducks every morning, and I recognize them as individuals (except when they bob bottoms up). There are also squabbling sea gulls, Brown Pelicans, Black-necked Stilts, and cormorants. Some of these birds hunt for prey from a position on the water, others dive into the water from the air to capture small fish and other food.

Near my houseboat a raft of fifty floating logs forms a bird habitat on which mostly gulls and cormorants rest. Because they don't have waterproofing oil, cormorants can dive deeply without being held up by excessive buoyancy. After swimming and diving for some time the cormorants rest on the logs and spread their water-logged wings to dry so they can dive again without sinking. All these birds are an integral part of the seascape; I watch them for hours with curiosity and amusement. When the black and white birds form up in a chorus line, extending their wings and vocalizing en mass, the choreography resembles a Broadway musical.

Because San Francisco Bay is on the pacific flyway it is a major stopover for migratory birds in winter: blizzards of geese, common loons, American Coots, Red Breasted Mergansers, Eared, Pied Billed, and Western Grebes, Belted Kingfishers and diving and dabbling ducks of all kinds, such as Canvass-backs, Tufted ducks, Scoters, and Mallards. I sit on my back deck for hours reading or trying to guess where diving cormorants or seals will surface. When I pass a neighbor's house at any time of day, an old, gray seagull named Waldo is likely to be perched on a railing near the front door waiting for the food my neighbor has been feeding it for a year.

Between November and March, especially in January, armies of herring surge through the Golden Gate from the ocean. Schools of these tasty fish make their way into Richardson Bay and spawn here, laying their gelatinous eggs on underwater rocks or vegetation. At such times tens of thousands of mixed flocks of different bird species fly together in formation past the houseboats, skimming a few inches above the water. They land in the relatively shallow Richardson Bay where adult herring and their eggs are concentrated and available. These eclectic, multitudinous flybys are a marvelous and stirring sight. The birds land and roil the water in a frenzy of feasting. And all this natural history, all these congregations of birds, especially, change all the time, throughout the day and seasonally.

As early as the 1880s people began mooring floating summer homes across from Sausalito in Belvedere Cove, Tiburon. These pleasure craft of wealthy San Franciscans were decked out with lanterns and pots of flowers and supported a water culture of leisure and sport. Families spent the week aboard rectangular flat bottomed "arks" while San Francisco's doctors, lawyers and bankers commuted to the city on steam-driven launches. Winter quarters for the arks were inland of the Corinthian Island Bridge. When the 1906 earthquake and fire destroyed much of San Francisco, the beached arks became emergency shelters for homeless families whose houses had been destroyed. The Depression brought an end to lavish entertaining aboard the arks and many of them became year-round rent free homes for the impoverished.

In the 1890s sportsmen built duck blinds on and off Sausalito's shores, some of which they very likely furnished with chairs and couches, perhaps even a bed, and some cooking equipment. Other early houseboats in the area were barges that were repaired on Sausalito mud flats, ca. 1914, by employees of the Argus Shipworks. These workers patched barges during the day and lived on or near them at night.

When the Golden Gate Bridge was completed, in 1937, some good old ferry boats were retired and beached at Gate Five of the shipyard, among them the *Charles Van Damme*, the *San Raphael,* and the *Issaquah.* Several of these paddle-wheel ferries, or parts of them, remain at Gate Five (otherwise the Gates Cooperative).

The real boom in waterfront (or on water) housing came during

World War II when the Marinship Shipyard employed 70,000 workers to build Liberty Ships. To construct the shipyard, the original Waldo Point itself was removed to create a waterfront cove. (To the eventual dismay and chagrin of county officials, the cove proved to also be a perfect home for houseboats). Since housing was scarce, some of these ingenious laborers created living quarters from old boats and any other materials they could scrounge. When the shipyard closed after the war, other boats such as scows, barges, dinghies, old navel craft and other floating equipment were added to the sometimes sinking floating waterfront collection.

After the war veterans and a number of the workers settled in the area, continuing the impecunious hand-to-mouth waterfront living tradition, enhanced by warm sunshine and calm breezes. Soon artists were attracted to this alternative lifestyle, followed by old beatniks, and young hippies. Water has always been a bohemian refuge and bohemians lived simply and frugally in order to buy time to follow their artistic and spiritual pursuits. While picturesque Sausalito had, from the early 1800's, always attracted weekend artists who crossed the Bay from San Francisco by sailboat, Sausalito swelled with artists and eccentrics during the post-war years. The rustic waterfront and growing houseboat community helped create a popular haven for creative persons and provided the foundation for the first Sausalito Arts Festival which took place in 1952.

The growing community of artists, writers, photographers, actors, film-makers, carpenters, seamstresses, craftspeople, and musicians (who formed a moderately successful band, the Red Legs) built owner-assembled dwellings without land costs, building permits, utility hook-ups or, ideally, store-bought building materials. Scavenging from what was already there, these squatters salvaged old hulls and topped them with millwork and hardware rescued and recycled from demolition sites and junk piles. In addition to various kinds of boats, they used pieces of arks, old windows and doors, stained glass, brass hinges, discarded furniture, scraps of metal and wood, porcelain fixtures, driftwood, lumber salvaged from the shipyard and put into communal piles, and the rich variety of other flotsam and jetsam common to all waterfronts. These free spirits practiced a kind of college educated primitivism combining self-denial with self-expression and inspired each other to new heights of funkiness. All kinds of living accommodations were fashioned in highly creative ways. Some Gates Cooperative houseboats were just plain shacks, usually of plywood; others were imaginative patched up live-in fantasy structures and sculptures.

So the story of the modern houseboats, as we know them today, began in earnest in the 1950s and 1960s and flourished in the 1970s when the Gate Five area became home to an Haight-Ashbury-like counter-culture, a seemingly anarchistic and chaotic haven for discontented sons and daughters of America's middle class who turned their creative talents to the challenge of living cheaply on the water and their resourcefulness into anti-establishment art. This group of houseboats became a cultural center and breeding ground for radicals, hippies, free-thinker, mystics, and bon vivants. Even those notorious bomb-happy revolutionaries from the Vietnam Era, the Weather Underground, went into hiding in the watery encampment and countercultural Neverland of the Sausalito houseboats.

From the start the house boater's creative anti-materialism was at odds with residents of expensive Sausalito hill homes who saw the houseboats as areas of poverty and urban blight. An accumulation of apparent junk lying around seemed to point to squalor and chaos. Few saw these houses as works of art, most saw them as eyesores.

In truth, the imaginative works of art the counter-culture created to live in wound up posing a health hazard to Richardson Bay. Thus, the Gates Community houseboats became the site of violent clashes with various state and local authorities who tried to remove them. None of the houseboats at Gate Five adhered to any sort building code, so officials offered a permanent birth in a new marina to any residents bringing their vessels up to safety codes and environmental standards. For those who complied (many did not) docks were built with hook-ups for water, gas, electricity and much needed sewer lines.

As a result of non-compliance the Gates Community has been almost constantly under siege. The Marin county supervisors struggled for a decade to resolve the ecological, safety, and what they thought were moral issues regarding these houseboats. In 1971 authorities condemned thirty floating homes and tried to remove them, resulting in the notorious "Battle of Richardson Bay" or "Houseboat Wars." The officials boarded a small Boston Whaler, glided surreptitiously into Gate Five, and towed out to sea a converted lifeboat hull belonging to artist Russell Grissom. Members of the community quickly formed a slapdash navel squadron of Chinese junks, canoes, rowboats and tugs and set off in hot pursuit. Sheriff's deputies jousted boat-to-boat with long-haired defenders. During the standoff and pushing and shoving between the authorities and the motley but courageous Gate Five fleet, Grissom and his boat were forgotten. Grissom spent the night aboard his boat and moved back to his mooring the next morning. In the end all houseboats were saved, their owners were charged $25 for reckless boat handling and the county declared a two-year moratorium. Those wars raged on the waterfront for a decade.

Among the more famous residents of the houseboats and defenders of their alternative lifestyle were the Zen philosopher, essayist and speaker Alan Watts, the abstract artist, collagist and color theorist Jean Varda, and the surrealist artist and founder of the Dynaton school of art Gordon Onslow-Ford. These three lived and worked on the *Vallejo,* a ferryboat decommissioned in 1949. Others the trio attracted included the actor, writer and sailor Sterling Hayden and the poet, cartoonist and lyricist Shel Silverstein. In 1977 Buckminster Fuller defended the squatting house boaters: "America has many groups of youths realistically living their attempt to rectify inequities outstanding in American life. They have attempted to educate their children in the simplicity of a century-ago pioneer America. The Waldo Point group in Sausalito…established their floating community on old boats, barges, floating homes, or shacks as a water colony. After a score of successful years of self-organization, they are now threatened with expulsion from their waterfront to make way for a rich middle-class houseboat marina."

The Gates Cooperative still exists as a small but dense area of thirty-eight houseboats which maintain the character of the original community. Here walkways between boats are planks or plywood which sag and tip, occasionally dipping into the water. Telephone wires and power lines are strung haphazardly (and hazardly) between leaning poles. The whole place looks exceedingly dilapidated, and exudes an atmosphere of poverty and mystery, even danger.

A special group of house boaters, related in philosophy, character and generally precarious economic status to the dwellers of the Gates Cooperative are the "anchor outs": those who live further off-shore, their often very bizarre dwellings moored in the sheltered waters of the middle of Richardson Bay. Some of these "houses" are just plain old boats, often drastically in need of repair, or living structures cobbled together on top of various derelict hulls. They are tethered to buoys sometimes chained to old car engines or other makeshift anchors sunk to the bottom. All have small watercraft, such as rubber rafts or rowboats swinging lazily in the water behind them, which are used to carry waste ashore or to get food, water, and fuel. I frequently see the anchor outs rowing to shore and returning, often with their dogs in the bow sniffing the breeze. While there have been anchor outs in Richardson Bay for more than one hundred years, the present ones are controversial and are catalysts for conflict with town and county authorities. New anchor outs are prohibited; those already there have been grandfathered into the houseboat community

After years of undetermined legal status, the future of the houseboats is secure. Houseboats are recognized as legitimate (and taxable) owned dwellings. Conventional mortgages and insurance are now relatively easy to obtain. And the seemingly never-ending conflicts over zoning laws, aesthetics, water rights and environmental issues have finally been resolved. According to a master plan some parking lots will be filled in and raised and the flooding bay water restrained by two to three feet retaining walls. Some of the thirty-eight homes of the Gates Cooperative will be brought up to code; more will be demolished and replaced with new models; twenty of these will be dispersed and placed into empty berths of the other marinas. A new short pier will be built in the lagoon between Issaquah and Liberty docks to accommodate the balance of the Gates Cooperative houseboats. And a green park will luxuriate between Gates Five and Six.

One of the many pleasures of living on the Sausalito floating homes are the potted flowers, shrubs, ferns, and small trees which line both sides of most common walkways and form virtual botanical gardens which emblazon the docks with kaleidoscopes of shimmering colors. There are many beautiful plants elegantly displayed by seemingly professional gardeners. These floral delights are grown in planters, (the only means of cultivation on the docks), and among them are fragrant roses of different colors, showy irises, New Zealand tea flowers, dahlias, geraniums, white, pink or purple clematis, rhododendrons with their trumpet-shaped flowers, and bougainvillea. Moonscapes of spiky cacti and smoother succulents can be seen in planters resting on tables and railings. Small trees such as palms, bonsai pines and Japanese maple add further variety. There are also climbing plants such as ivies, trumpet vines, potato vines, grapes, and blue, purple or white wisteria, as well as fruit bearing trees including mandarin oranges, lemon and lime trees. In addition there are herbs such as basil, oregano, Australian Rosemary, sweet woodruff, lemon grass and borage. It is rumored, and almost certainly true, that marijuana plants are cultivated somewhere among the Waldo Point docks. Vegetables such as zucchini, eggplant, cherry tomatoes and bell peppers are also grown. Butterflies flutter among the plants and finches, hosts of sparrows and shimmers of humming birds hover and fly around in the gardens. Drip irrigation is a necessity but many houseboat gardeners hand-water most evenings while their neighbors congregate at the house for daily news, gossip or general conversation.

While the containers are mostly pots, I find flowers growing in an old leather shoe, a painted ceramic toad, a wine barrel, a plastic bowl. Closer scrutiny of the gardens reveals other little surprises: a half hidden pink carved wooden elf peering out from underneath the foliage, a cutout painted cow, a metal fish, a bobbing dime-store duck. There are also flowering trellises, homemade fountain displays, imaginative dreamscapes of windmills, and water-spraying tilt-a-whirls. House boaters regard their gardens as works of color, form and emotion, and each garden, designed from the bottom up, declares a preference. Other plants, flowers, and small trees are seen on rooftop decks or on the floating docks appended to the backs of the homes. And hanging plants such as Wandering Jew and Spider Plants are suspended inside and out.

Docks are the best way to organize houseboats into neighborhoods equipped with municipal services and most residential docks are wooden boardwalks supported by timber or steel pilings. There are different mooring configurations and the docks are like faces: the physiognomy of the dock reveals its personality. The two relatively new piers (East and West) of Kappas Marina run parallel to the shore and are laid out regularly with sparse use of vegetation. The houseboats there, evenly spaced, orderly and clean cut, reveal themselves in one view, like a suburban street lined with houses in pre automobile days. All other docks are perpendicular to the shoreline, and each forms its own neighborhood. Some of these moorings are more abstruse, like convoluted old towns, winding or rectangular but not predictable. There may be logic to their design but it is not immediately understood. In addition to Kappas Marina and to the Gates Cooperative Community, there are six other docks or marinas, each with different characteristics and vibes and each displaying their own arrangements of flowers and plants.

Issaquah dock, the most floral, is resplendent with adjacent plants down both sides of the entire length of its boardwalk, forming a lush linear garden of great variety and beauty. The Issaquah walkway itself is narrow and the organic process of daily close encounters between its residents makes Issaquah dock especially lively and communal: its residents evidently believe that the more plants the merrier the place. There is also a strong presence of Asia there: Buddhist icons and symbols and other Eastern spiritual paraphernalia, spirit houses to welcome one's ancestors. Gate Six and a Half is the northern most dock, set off more or less by itself. It has large evenly spaced concrete planters faced with small stones. Yellow Ferry dock is named after and was built expressly to accommodate the large old yellow-painted ferry boat at its far end, complete with tall smokestack and wooden paddle wheel, now resting quietly as a floating home. Yellow Ferry dock is an elaborately configured pier but with only a few plants set in permanent wooden planters. The short A Dock has only single-story houses. Liberty Dock has some trellises and small potted trees, but not much in the way of flowers or other vegetation. Main Dock has a lot of flowers and shrubs grouped in self-contained oasis-like clusters with large unadorned spaces between them. South Forty is a wide dock (about twelve feet across) which extends far out into the bay and has large pots of shrubs outside its railings on specially constructed wooden stands. Half-way up its length the dock widens into a diamond shape furnished with wooden benches for use as a common area. South Forty then branches off into smaller docks each reached by long ramps. Some of the branches end in deck platforms planted and furnished as common spaces for pods of two or three houseboats. Liberty Dock and Issaquah Dock have right-angled elbow extensions at their bay ends, turning to the left and right respectively, so that a single-entranced lagoon is enclosed between them.

There about 450 floating homes in the Sausalito houseboat community. Their architecture is exceptionally diverse, colorful and funky. The newer, more conventional, houseboats resemble landed homes in style and construction, but for the most they are small—like doll houses—ordinary homes in miniature, but with more glass: skylights, portholes, overly large windows, glass walls and doors—particularly out back where they open directly to water. Since they are small, like tight ships where every space counts, many have lofts as well as built in bookcases and other built-ins.

Some houseboats seem to have sprung out of bizarre dreams, others conform to or distort the hulls of the old ships they are built upon. Issaquah Dock has a strong presence of Asia: statues of Buddha, Buddhist icons and symbols, Eastern spiritual paraphernalia, spirit houses to welcome one's ancestors. The water dwellings of Sausalito are entered from the docks by way of ramps or gang planks. At high tide, the houseboats rise above the docks, at low tide they sink below. Thus their aspects change as one either ascends or descends the ramps.

In addition to conventional-looking homes, houseboats fall into several other categories: *exotic,* reflecting the owner's travel and cultural interests, such as a reproduced Japanese barn and other Asian dwellings; *boxes,* of little or no design and providing minimal shelter; *sculpture,* striking all-over designs, artistic forms employing octagons and many other shapes which just happen also to be floating homes; *assemblages,* thrown together, jerry-built patchwork style from a variety of materials; *vehicles* of all kinds converted to living quarters—mobile homes, for instance, attached to floating bases, World War II landing craft, lifeboats, tugs and other boats, a VW microbus within a floating dinghy; and a few *showplaces,* such as the 3,000 square foot, four-story "*Dragon Boat*" with four bedrooms, three and a half baths, a living room with an 18 foot vaulted ceiling, and a chef's gourmet kitchen. *The Dragon Boat* towers over other homes and would be luxurious even on land. Among the names other houseboats are *Tranquility Base, The Big Picture, The Answer, Freedom,* and *Chateau Bateau.* Virtually all houseboats have floating docks of various sizes behind or beside them, as well as one or more decks, including rooftop decks.

With a few exceptions, the Sausalito floating homes are constructed of wood and are expressions of the personalities and interests of their owners, particularly in their painted colors and interior and exterior decoration. There is liberal use of stained glass and frosted glass incorporating abstract designs or >semi-realistic figures; also collages, portholes, model yachts, brass fittings, ship's bells and ships wheels, barometers, bas relief, signs (**to the beach >**), compasses, ship's propellers, and other nautical stuff, including pilot houses of old ferries. Fish nets, flags, pennants and ensigns, colored buoys, ropes, old bottles, paddles and oars, model birds and decoys, and small statuary are displayed on railings, balustrades and floating docks. I lived for a while on the *Painted Whale* whose door was guarded by a bust of Joseph Conrad. Houseboats also use unorthodox materials rarely seen in landed houses: bamboo, teak, fiberglass, mahogany, cedar shingles, and stainless, galvanized, rusted or painted steel. And they are often painted in wild colors: lavender, Flamingo Pink, turquoise, orange, lipstick red, robin's egg blue, magenta, or combinations of these and other colors.

As opposed to landed homes, which usually conform to norms and thus reject artistic experimentation, water inspires artistic license and some houses are like public art installations. One of the most unusual and original of these is *Train Wreck* which looks like a railroad car has crashed into a house. *Train Wreck* is built around an 1889 North Pacific Pullman car severed in half and its two segments turned at right angles to each other and lowered onto a concrete barge. Then a house was built around and over it, exposing some of the car to the outside and enveloping the rest. Half the car has become dining room and kitchen and retains its original mahogany paneling, as well as original windows and brass fixtures; the other half, the old sleeping compartment, has become a living room. The master bedroom occupies the entire bottom floor, and the third floor of this highly imaginative dwelling rises at angles into a glassy, modernist eagles-nest study with 360 degree views. *Train Wreck* has a complex aesthetic which incorporates both historic preservation and the traditions of conceptual art. Another unusual design is *The Owl,* a tall houseboat built in the 1970s over the top of an abandoned pile driver. *The Owl's* strange upper story has a concave roofline with a triangular peak in the middle and two large round windows. This odd superstructure resembles the head of an owl and is encircled by a widows-walk.

Other Sausalito houseboats are every size, shape and description: from elegant, if conventional, floating homes to medium-sized hand-crafted houses that look like floating sculpture, to unique water-shanties simply thrown together, to actual boats either transformed by creating more living space or simply left as boats. Three of this latter type are the *S. S. Maggie,* an old steam-schooner that was converted into a home in the 1930s; the *Mirene,* a pristine tugboat built in the early 1900s and seemingly still operational today; and *Go-getter,* a restored wooden logging boat. On South Forty is a World War II landing craft retrofitted with canted walls. In size, shape and headroom this ten by thirty-six foot boat is a rectangular tube of minimal space lined with built-ins and no fancier than a mobile home.

A further type of dwelling, non-floating and on the land end of some docks, are the large, century-old aforementioned "arks." The remaining arks are among the original old hand-crafted floating homes but they have been placed onto pilings, and are now affixed to the shoreline. Arks are typically rectangular structures with slightly pitched roofs which extend over all-around decks. *The Mayflower,* which was "landed" ca. 1920-1930, is a fine example of original ark design. It has retained its original redwood paneling, windows and doors, claw-foot bathtub, and portal windows. Another ark, the *Montgomery,* is a Tiburon train station which was wheeled down to the bay and hoisted atop a molasses barge on which she still sits today.

While there are several types of houseboat flotation, including hulls of old shallow-draft boats, steel buoys or barrels, Styrofoam, and logs, most houseboats in Sausalito are floated by custom-made buoyant concrete barges (platforms) or concrete hulls. Portland cement, which does not dissolve under water, is reinforced with steel bars; these foundations rely on Archimedes' statement that anything can float if it is shaped to displace its own weight in water. A barge is about a four feet deep concrete slab engineered to fit the dimensions and weight of the particular house it supports. Barges carry all the livable space above the water. Hulls, partly submerged and watertight, are one big air chamber which float in such a way that the lower floor of a two-story houseboat is below the waterline. The barges and hulls of houseboats are attached, or moored, to pilings in such a way that they move up and down with the tide. Most houseboats are slightly tilted for drainage, with sump pumps at their lowest corner.

The Sausalito houseboat marinas, with their patchwork of architectural styles and periods, create an exceptional sense of visual excitement quite unlike anything I have ever experienced.

Movement is the world of difference between living in an onshore landed house and dwelling in a houseboat on and in the water. My houseboat is a perch on a sweeping plane much wider and grander than that upon which a house on land sits. It is a floating observations station: an outpost or field station looking out onto a fascinating, ever changing kinetic water-meadow with sky reflected.

In the bay, sounds, sights, light, and water are affected by movement. The moving surface of water changes everything. On top of the water there is a sensation of subtle and unpredictable movement, especially since the wind, too, changes force and direction as the land warms and cools during the day. Sometimes the movement is nearly imperceptible, other times, when walloped by nature, the houseboats rock and roll like teacups in a tempest and hanging plants, fern pots, lamps, or wind chimes swing like pendulums. One stormy night I woke to the sound of champagne glasses breaking on the kitchen floor. The long-stemmed glasses had been shaken loose from the ceiling rack from which they had dangled. On houseboats the vagaries of changing weather are dramatic and insistent and one adapts to the alternating rhythms of the water which are effected by wind, tide and current. Even on calm days, when there is little surface movement, birds and boats travel in the water and either make the houseboats move or create the impression that they are moving. The water changes from hardly moving at all at slack tide to wavelets quietly slapping against hulls of houseboats to whitecaps or tide rips when current and wind are opposing each other. Sometimes you see the movement, in a swaying lamp for instance, but don't feel it; sometimes you feel the movement but don't see it. Smaller houseboats bob in delightful ways and the motion of the water is energizing. The movement puts my body on full alert, electrifies all multi-sensory neuromuscular systems, and reminds me how really sensitive are our inner ears, eyes, feet and toes.

Water residents love water with a passion all but incomprehensible to those who don't share it. To house boaters water is not an alien environment but an alternative atmosphere akin to liquid air. I love the changing moods of water in a shallow bay, even more so when it is joined by the reflected movement of clouds.

Sounds, too, are unique on floating homes: the creaks and groans of houseboats straining against their moorings, footfalls drumming on the wooden planks of the docks, the chafing of gangplanks on walkways, the calls of birds, the rustling of garden plants stirring in the wind, the singing and whistling of the wind itself through the rigging of nearby sailboats. Rain pattering on the docks or splattering into the bay also sounds different than on land.

> Oh, the houseboats are a marvelous place,
> Where the people look you straight in the face.
> Life here is so good that it mystifies,
> And men without ties have smiles in their eyes.
> Everyone does just whatever they choose,
> And the girls keep pairs of red high-heeled shoes
> (To dance off the very rare houseboat blues).

Just before I left the houseboats to stay at the Veteran's Administration Mental Health ward, I got very depressed and bought a pistol: a Beretta .32. I was obsessed with the pistol and kept it loaded with a clip in it and pointed it at my head a lot. I finally threw it in the bay, but the water was clear and shallow so I got it back and cleaned it up and wiped if off. Then I brought it to the VA and kept it hidden in the car. After a while, I put it into a waterproof bag and buried. It stayed there for several weeks until I finally recovered the pistol and deep-sixed back the bay. The trouble with trying to kill yourself is that you might not, you might just be mutilated and become a paraplegic!

Urinalysis

My squash partner, Jack, who is retired now, enjoys a good joke. All the more so when it's at the expense of someone else. He is a San Francisco lawyer and shares a secretary with one of his partners whose office is next to his. Jack's partner, Kenneth, a pleasant enough man and good lawyer, is fastidious, a little stuffy, a dandy who chooses his high-priced clothing carefully.

Kenneth has some fine silk ties which he sends out for cleaning to a special French Laundry in Los Angeles. On day Jack intercepted the package of ties being returned from the laundry, razored open the package, put his partner's clean ties in his own desk drawer, substituted some dingy old ties of his own, and carefully resealed the box. When Kenneth opened the box he was visibly upset. He showed the ties to his secretary, exclaiming loudly that they weren't his and that the laundry had really screwed up. He then returned the ties to the laundry with a pointed note. A few days later the laundry called him and said they have never seen the ties before.

Jack's partner also has dress shirts specially hand made to his measurements in Bologna, Italy. The shirts, which cost about $350 each, have long white collars with edge stitching, white French cuffs, single needle tailoring with silk thread, and double thick mother-of-pearl buttons. He is particularly fond of these shirts and of their maker Andino Benvenuti. One day Jack went to Chinatown and bought a Chinese newspaper printed on one side only. As before, with the ties, Jack intercepted a package of three shirts, opened it and inserted pieces of the newspaper into the breast pocket of each. Then he carefully resealed the package and put it back into Kenneth's mail. The next day his partner came to work saying loudly "Aha, I caught those damned guys—they have their shirts made in China. Imagine the markup they must get!"

But Jack's coup de grace was the office chair caper. Kenneth has expensive furnishing in his office, including the comfortable desk chair he works in. It is dark blue leather stuffed with PU foam made of one hundred percent cotton fabric and there are zippered openings in the leather in back of the chair so the stuffing can be replaced if necessary. Jack ordered a box of urinal cakes used to deodorize urinals in men's restrooms from Fresh Products, Inc in Toledo, Ohio. He stayed late one evening, unzipped two of the openings in the chair and inserted two urinal cakes. These deodorizers slowly dissolve in air so that his partner's chair let off a peculiar but familiar smell. To make matters worse, one of the chemicals in this brand of urinal cake deadens the olfactory nerves so that after a while, because he sat in the chair most of the day, Kenneth lost his sense of smell. But valuable clients and others who came into his office noticed a strong, pungent odor which they were too polite to mention. After a week or so, someone in the firm brought the smell to Kenneth's attention. Although he couldn't smell it himself, he had the chair sent back to the manufacturer, but not before Jack had removed the urinal cakes. The manufacturer, of course, found nothing wrong with the chair and returned it to the law firm. Upon the chair's arrival, Jack immediately inserted new cakes. Someone complained of the smell again and the chair was returned to the maker a second time, minus the offensive inserts. The chair maker again found nothing wrong and returned the chair to Jack's partner. At this point Jack confessed to the prank. But what will he do to his poor beleaguered partner next?

Mean Streets

We tread with sorrow down mean streets
where poverty with hunger meets;
alert to each poor soul we pass,
we know them as the underclass.

These poor once had dreams like ours
of trees and homes, gardens and cars;
but now they are so destitute
they eat the rind of rotten fruit.

Their skin is raw, their eyes are red,
we see them hopeless, nearly dead;
these are the poor, the homeless ones
who live on waste and moldy buns.

Their teeth are missing, swollen gums;
these are the ones that some call bums.
Devastated, swollen faces;
tragedies in public places.

These are the weary, the wary, the hurt,
poor souls who live in pain and dirt.
Some have been by madness taken.
All are forgotten, all forsaken.

Their clothes are filthy, worn and torn,
they curse the days that they were born.
They pass around the drug-filled needle

and itch and scratch at lice and beetle.

They grieve in alleys and doorways,
and suffer all their nights and days.
They live upon the streets by stealth,
and have no stable mental health.

These are the damaged, the all cut up
who, shaking, hold the blind man's cup.
These are the lost, the poor, the sick
who sleep upon the cold, hard brick.

The homeless—they are me and you:
Protestant, Catholic, Atheist, Jew.
There are streets like these are wherever we go.
How do they endure these streets of woe?

There's poverty throughout our land,
a land that once we thought was grand
"Life, liberty and happiness?"—
for the homeless is a hopeless wish.

America's the richest country on earth
and yet there seems to be a dearth
of real compassion for the poor
who need our help more and more.

Where are the wealthy, where are the rich?
To help these shades out of Hell's ditch.
They're trapped in chaos and distress—
we love them more, not love them less.

These are the homeless, the hollow men

who haunt our dreams again and again.
These are the millions, who live in Hell,
these are the homeless we know too well.

Oh my God, what have we done?
We have ignored the homeless one!
Oh my God, how poverty thrives!
Give us the love to change their lives

The Presidio of San Francisco

Imagine the soldiers of three nations
at their duty stations;
summon up the Presidio's former commandants,
their names echoed in the names of San Francisco streets:
Anza, Moraga, Sal, Arguello;
San Vincente, Sanchez, Martinez, Vallejo;
Funston, Sumner, Stillwell, Mason.
Listen to the buglers of the past:
the rapid staccato of reveille played fast,
the slow mellow mournful sounds of taps,
the mess call's quick rat-a-tat-tat.
Hear the tramp of boots on the parade grounds;
see the sentries making their rounds.
Listen to the shrill commands of drill sergeants:
"Right Dress!" "Parade Rest!" "Dis-Missed!"
Hear the slap of hands on hardwood stocks at rifle drill;
see the rifles stacked cone-like during field exercises.
Hear the clinking of whisky and beer glasses and
smell the gray eye-stinging haze of cigarette smoke
in the Officers' and Enlisted Men's Clubs.
Hear the chatter and din of feeding soldiers

and the clanking of plates and utensils in the mess halls.
See the dress uniforms at the Army's birthday balls.
See officers playing polo and hear
the smack of wooden mallets on wooden balls.
See and hear the mock battle staged
by the California National Guard
on July 3, 1876.

See the troopers plant 100,000 trees and shrubs
in 1886, and many more later.
See and feel the flames, choking smoke, and searing heat
of the fatal fire that destroyed General Pershing's house
and killed his wife and daughters
while he was chasing Poncho Villa in Mexico.
See the horse-drawn howitzers
and caissons of the Field Artillery;
see the Coast Artillery at their shore battery bunkers,
in wide-brimmed campaign hats and gaiters,
and hear the boom and rumbling thunder
batteries' big guns.
See the soldiers, bayonets fixed,
trying to keep order in San Francisco
after the great earthquake and fire of 1906;
see the tent-camps in the Presidio
for civilians displaced from the city.

Hear the buzz of slow-flying airplanes
over Crissy Field in the 1920s and see
the daredevil stunts of "Bird-Boy" Smith.
And, finally, see the last forest-green troop-trucks
pass out through the Presidio's Lombard Gate
when the army finally decided to vacate.

In the auspicious year 1776,
Spain, in its fading glory suspicious of
the ambition of British and Russian fur traders,
sent Captain Juan Bautista de Anza,
in his blue and red uniform and cloak,
to establish a Presidio at the northernmost point
of the Spanish Empire in America.
Although strategically at the mouth of a bay
that one of Anza's officers described as
"…a marvel of nature…a harbor of harbors…"
the red and gold flag of Spain flew over a desolate site:
scrubby shrubs, sand dunes, marsh and swamp near the shore,
foul winter weather, severe storms.
In 1792 Vancouver
described the Presidio as
"…a square area whose sides were of 200 yards in length
enclosed by a mud wall resembling a pound for cattle."
The Spanish garrison was never ready to do battle.

When Mexico gained independence from Spain
in 1821, Mexicans took over the Presidio
which deteriorated further under its red and green flag.
Twenty years later a U. S. Naval officer wrote
"…we were scarcely able to distinguish the Presidio…
The buildings were deserted, the walls had fallen to decay,
the guns were dismounted, and everything around it lay in quiet."

In 1846,
at the start of the Mexican-American War,
Americans occupied the undefended Presidio -
Where the stars and stripes have flown ever since.
The Presidio swelled with soldiers during
the wars against the Western Indians,

the Spanish-American War, World Wars I and II.
As a training and embarkation post
for wars in the Pacific, the Presidio,
often studded with temporary tent camps,
became one of the most important U. S. Army bases.
During the Spanish-American War
80,000 soldiers passed through it
on the way to the Philippines;
during World War II 1,500,000 soldiers
embarked from the Presidio.

See the remains of the oldest building in San Francisco:
the adobe walls of a Spanish commandant's house
built long ago, now enclosed within the later walls
of the Officers' Club.
See the two bronze cannon
cast in Lima, Peru in 1673
and brought to the Presidio under Spanish rule.
See one of the finest existing
Civil War masonry forts at Fort Point.
See the varied architectural styles
of the Presidio's 800 white buildings:
Federal and the Colonial Revival,
Queen Anne, Spanish Mission Revival
Mediterranean Revival, and other styles.
Designated a National Historic Landmark
in 1963, and now transformed from
military post to national park,
the San Francisco Presidio
has a renowned collection
of classic 19th and 20th century
military architecture.

In the middle of a great city,
the Presidio, groomed and pretty,
is a captivating oasis
of sylvan forests of Monterey Pines and Cypress,
Blue-Gum Eucalyptus, Palms, and other trees,
grassy playing fields, picnic areas and camp grounds,
and hiking trails and hill tops with splendid panoramic views.
Enjoy Inspiration Point, Mountain Lake,
Lobos Creek Valley, the Coastal Bluffs,
Baker and Marshall Beaches, and other inspiring features.
Deer are found within its grounds,
as well as many other creatures such as
foxes, coyotes, quail, wild turkey, and red-tailed hawks.
Go see the Presidio's residential neighborhoods,
where the living is rural, lazy and slow:
among them Infantry Terrace, Pilots Row,
Kobbe Terrace, Simonds Loop, Riley Row.

On the south shore of a beautiful Bay,
the Presidio is a grand urban public park today,
a landmark replete with military history and
significant and meaningful symbols and experiences;
a pastoral place of nourishing nature,
a refuge for those seeking renewal,
a quiet spacious arboreal jewel.

My Vasculitis

In July 2013 I became ill: chronic pain in the muscles (mostly below the waist), extreme fatigue, chills in the evening, fever at night with night sweats, slight runny nose and cough It got worse, not better.

I saw Dr. Kerstin Morehead (a rheumatologist) for first time. More blood tests; also a CT scan with contrast. A few days later I had a bone marrow biopsy. Things remained the same or getting worse.

I don't remember when I had the stroke, but I think it was July 14. I have a vague recollection of when I had the two seizures. I recall trying to get to the bathroom, twisting and turning, finally going down. Fortunately, my wife was with me and alert. She caught me and called 911; the small fire truck came and took me to California Pacific Medical Center where I was deposited in the emergency room.

I shared a room was on the fifth floor with another man who was waiting for a kidney transplant and needed dialysis. He went downstairs for it about 6:00 PM and stayed there for about three hours. After a while I was sent to the ICU on the third floor. That was a wild place, the nurses constantly talking about parties they were going to have. No one in their right mind would want to be and ICU nurse. I was there for three days, and then was sent back upstairs and given a room without a roommate. I remember Patrick, but I called him Michael or Louis; I couldn't get his name straight, although I did better with his assistant. There was a doctor in the ICU I didn't like very much.

I was heavily medicated, especially with steroids and experienced steroid narcosis which made my cry every time someone I liked called. And I took about 20 other medications which I am still taking, although I've cut down on the steroids, thank heavens.

There are many kinds of Vasculitis and it is extremely difficult to diagnose. I had about every test and procedure in the book, not to speak of many blood test and urine test. My type is Anca's Vasculitis which is very rare: about one in a million persons get it. Most doctors thought it was Polymyalgia Rheumatitus. I asked Dr. Morehead if she had ever had as difficult a diagnosis and she said no.

I had to urinate every half hour and had difficulty keeping my robe dry. It was a hassle. One peculiar thing about vasculitis is that your feet have a kind of edema: they swell up and tingle on the bottom and you have no feeling in them. This happened in the beginning and makes it hard to walk, so today I am unsteady. The left foot is worse than the right.

In spite of the doctors and nurses being nice, I hated the hospital: The constant noise at night, the interruptions, the inability to sit upright, the urination, the inability to read most of the time. One of the doctors wouldn't let me go home. At one point I decided to go anyway, dressed in wet clothes, and almost made it out of there. I was prohibited by the doctors to leave and stopped by a guard. When I did leave it was 9:00 o'clock at night.

I had several visitors, my psychotherapist and a friends. My sons and wife were there constantly. I don't know what I would have done without them. They were a great help, both to my spirits and physically.

I was in the hospital for fourteen days. After coming home, I climbed the twenty-nine stairs at our place with difficulty. Then I had home care: a young man named Michael and another named Scott, both pleasant people. And also a physical therapist who didn't last very long. There was also a nurse and a nutritionist who would come to see me, all of course at my own expense. The nurse lasted about a month.

I am on a very restricted diet of low carbohydrates, no sugar, no sodium and no phosphorous. Fortunately my wife is a very good cook. I fell twice: once when going into my wife's pocket book and tore the left toenail off, another time I tripped but there was no damage.

So now I am home and getting slowly better. I'm going sailing for the first time in six months. And I'm going to join a gym for exercise. That's my experience with Vasculitis.

The Princess Tree

From my sick-room bed I see
my neighbor's lovely Princess tree
whose fragrance wafts into my room
dispelling many thoughts of gloom.

Its five-starred blossoms seem to me
to bravely bloom perpetually;
pure purple flower and heart-shaped leaf
bring to my distraught mind relief.

This tree, that bright and constant glows,
soothes my cares and daily woes
and brings to me comfort and calm
by quieting concern and qualm.

Tree-trimmers come with sharpened shears
and cut off branches with their flowers;
yet I am not sorrowful, I don't shed tears:
I know this tree's self-healing powers.

Now, when in tranquil repose,
or when I sleep and dream, I see
the purple-passioned Princess tree
blazing forth its destiny,
so that even in the darkest night
it shines on me its brightest light.

If this stout-hearted tree can stand fast,
rooted in sandy soil and crumbling rock,
and can withstand cold, cut, shock and windy blast,
and still flourish in the storm's fiercest eye…

Then so, I know, can I.

I dated several women in San Francisco, a Russian woman and an American who was an artist. I also corresponded, via the internet, with a woman in Berkeley and told her I'd go and see her. But she said she was a transvestite so I declined.

I went to the Veterans Administration Medical Center in San Francisco because I was depressed again. They gave me a psychiatrist I didn't like, but eventually I got another one who was much better. I stayed in the mental health building upstairs. The place was run like a homeless shelter: out by seven in the morning, back in by five. Again they wanted to me to do ECT, but I refused. One time I got stuffed up and had to wear a catheter for a few days. I got a good lawyer from Swords to Plowshares downtown and he eventually got me full disability. As such I get about $5,000 per month. And I wrote this poem:

At the San Francisco VA Medical Center

"…federal property…weapons and drugs
prohibited…video surveillance…"

At 7:30 am, and all day,
at the San Francisco VA,
they straggle from the # 45 bus
and wobble like sickly drunks,
some with walkers or canes.
Wheelchairs can be had.

Others come in
red, white, and blue service vans stenciled
"All gave some, some gave all."

Don't make eye contact
with the crazy lady
babbling nonsense
to herself;
she doesn't need you for talking.

Keep away from the snarly man
with the hair-trigger temper and gunmetal eyes
who's let out daily from lock-up.

But the short round with spiky beard
and tattoos on his bald head
is no one to dread.

When a vet with a catheter
shuffles by,
urine sloshing in his leg bag,
pretend not to hear it.

An old sergeant in pajamas,
with throat cancer
smokes a cigarette,
or two or three butts,
and stops from time to time
to breathe from his oxygen bottle,
then wheezes and coughs.

The big dude with dreadlocks,
brown, gapped teeth,
five gold-plated chains and silver bracelets,
fishes a cigarillo from his pocket.
His t-shirt may say
"Vietnam Vet."
or "Screw you."

When the smoking cessation group lets out
The brothers gather
(some in camouflage uniforms)
praise the program,
then light up and
bum cigarettes from each other
or pass them from mouth to mouth;
A honky spits a goober on the concrete:
splat.

The substance abusers have a bummy smell:
tobacco, alcohol, armpits, unwashed clothes.
"Whazzup up, man? You jus chillin' dude? How yo Mama?"
Greetings, not questions,
spoken blankly, eyes dull.

The homeless,
backpacks holding all they own,
change clothes or clean up
in the restrooms
and idle or sleep,
without appointments,
in the waiting rooms of the clinics,
or congregate outside
talking of shelters and jail.
Some come every day:
(the weary, the wary, the hurt,
those who live in pain and dirt).
The VA is their digs
their refuge,
their off-street community.

Half a man goes through the sliding doors
holding his shiny steel arms and hands

high in a V
(for violence?)
and limps on his prosthetic leg.

Code blue sounds
a flat-liner
revealing the persistence
of death—
the aura of which not even dense fog
can diffuse.

These people
fought for their country,
or would have.
God bless America.
God bless America.

Stow Lake, Golden Gate Park, San Francisco

Before crossing Fulton Street to the Rose Garden
in Golden Gate Park
I tuck my parrot, Streak,
safely under my jacket.
Might jump into traffic. Almost lost her once.

Late spring. The Garden is an emblazoned
botanical candy shop
of fragrant kaleidoscopic shimmering colors:
butter yellow, purple, reds, apricot, orange, pink, white,
other colors. Some of these queens of flowers,
including densely clustered floribundas, are labeled
Mardi Gras, Dream Come True, Sans Souci, Sheer Bliss,
Roman Holiday, Mystic Beauty, Rainbow Knockouts.

A rose is a rose is a rose. Smells sweet by any name.
Streak, now on my shoulder,
a burst of color too—green, yellow, blue, burnt-umber -
bobs her head comically to passersby.

We cut through a fence of rose-laden trellises
to a secluded bowl-shaped field perfect for picnics,
then across a larger field strewn with small portable soccer goals
for practice when the nearby grammar school lets out.
Used to play soccer. Great game.

We cross JFK drive
to the cr-r-uck, c-r-uck, cr-r-ucking of ravens.
Tricksters in Indian mythology. Smart.

Moving up Stow Lake Drive
we pass a California Pepper Tree,
several reddish-pink flowered New Zealand Tea trees,
pockets of gay wildflowers, flowering shrubs,
carefully planted flower-beds,
and ferns such as Western Lady Fan.
Wish I knew more about flowers and trees.
In Florida, when I was five,
fell out of a Banyan tree. Broke my arm.

The grassy areas of the park
are pock-marked by dirt-mounds of gopher holes;
the little brown burrowing buck-toothed creatures
are hard to see, but there's one
near the sidewalk darting its head back and forth
like a soldier in a foxhole overcome by curiosity
but refusing to come fully out.

Streak and I pass the bicycle rental office
on the way to the boathouse and snack shop
where elderly from the neighborhood
hang out on benches overlooking the lake.
I often see the same man
taking pictures from the west bank
in a spot where still water reflects foliage, birds float,
and Strawberry Hill is framed between Cypress trees.
The fascination of water, gently rippling, restful.
Birds so tame.
Most of the colored paddle boats and green row boats
are tied up; on weekends they are much in use
by lovers, or by families.
I love sailing in San Francisco Bay.
Scary wind sometimes.
The water birds, especially gulls, geese, and Mallard ducks
whose males are gaudy -
Gaudeamus igitur…Juvenes dum sumus -
congregate near the boathouse
and squabble over thrown bits and pieces.
Streak regards her feathered cousins with curiosity.

Stow Lake is a moat: it surrounds
Strawberry Hill
which can be crossed to by two bridges:
the simple Roman Bridge
or the rough-stoned double-arched Rustic Bridge.
Strolling around the lake,
on a path originally used for horse-drawn carriages,
we see an occasional squirrel,
a single blue-jay, a robin or two, some cowbirds.
As a kid, I shot birds and squirrels.
With a .22. Yuck!
Until I grew ashamed of the blood and guts.

A Canadian goose perches on a shore-rock
standing sentry over its gaggle of fluffy goslings;
further on a paddling of under soft ducks dip, bottoms up
like bathtub toys,
in the nourishment-laden
soupy pea-green water tinged with emerald.
Should have been an ornithologist.
Bird man of Stow Lake.

I take Streak off my shoulder
and we rest on a bench while she
scuttles sideways along the backrest
as I gaze in awe at a slate-colored Great Blue Heron
standing on one leg, silent, stately, composed.
Guten tag mein herren.

We move along and see
more than a dozen western pond turtles
on a half-submerged log.
The turtles crane their dark-brown necks to the sun;
Their deep- olive shells seem like stepping stones to heaven.

School children, fascinated with Streak, approach us.
I encourage her to talk English
but she just bobs and weaves, pins her eyes, jabbers and croons.
Hey, bird. Can you talk?
Yeah, I can talk. Can you fly?

We cross over the Rustic Bridge to Strawberry Hill
and walk eastward along the shore -
what is so appealing about islands? -
to the Chinese Peace Pavilion.
Ah Buddhism! So sane, so sensible,

so psychological. Om Mani Padme Hum.

The pavilion, dark red pillars,
bluish-green glazed tile roof, marble stools,
ornately painted arabesque ceiling panels
with dragon motifs, is a quiet place
near the steady splosh of Huntington Falls.
People get married at the Falls,
a place of glistening spiritual quietude
where water drops 75 feet and
flows into the lake over flat gray stones.
Snowy egrets wade here,
far whiter than milk or cotton
or a white wedding dress.
Streak and I linger in this numinous place.

Then we climb to the top of the hill
where I put Streak on a branch
and take in the 360 degree views:
the city, the ocean, the Golden Gate Bridge, Mount Tamalpais.
Can see the Farallones on a good day, they say.
On the way back down beside the Falls,
I put Streak on the iron banister which she slides down
until, losing balance, she flies to my shoulder.
We enjoy this and do it several times.
What would I do without this silly,
playful bird I am so fond of?
And what she without me?

We walk north from the Falls over the Roman Bridge,
then east along the north end of the lake
where a clutch of gulls, ducks and geese are feeding
on bread and popcorn.

A pair of Brown Pelicans fly past
like two old front-heavy Boeing Stratocruisers.
Pelicans are my other favorite birds.

Leaving the lake, we take a path
that winds through English Ivy ground cover, small palms,
purplish-blue wildflowers,
flowering cherry trees.
In a glade, a stand of Yew trees
How do you do, yew? It's me and Streakadoo
and a fan-leaved Ginkgo tree.
Gingko. Oldest plant on earth. Living fossil.

Streak and I re-cross JFK Drive at the Rose Garden,
go right and descend into the Hollow which
lies between the Drive and Fulton Street.
The Hollow, a calm and soothing woody place
is a deeply-shaded natural temple of tall Monterey Pines
and camphor-scented Blue Gum Eucalyptus;
a lush grove whose soft dappled ground is strewn
with fallen branches and trunks and criss-crossed by dirt paths.
I feel whole here. At peace.
Streak is riding backwards now;
I see and feel her tail near my left cheek.

We climb up the side of the Hollow.
I put Streak under my jacket to cross Fulton Street again.
For me and my fine feathered friend,
our walk has come to an end.

Furniture

My ex-wife got the antique furniture
we'd collected over the years.
So I bought furniture from IKEA.

When I remarried my new wife and I merged two households.
After two months my furniture began to disappear:
the three dun colored Billy bookcases ($34.79 each)
were set out on the street;
my Torsby/Nandor dining table
found its disassembled way into the garage;
I saw the Bekväm step stool ($19.99) and
the Bosse natural wood kitchen stool ($24.99)
in the Salvation Army when I was there looking for books;
the birch Ekby Oxie coffee table ($50.99) Don't know?;
she sold the six dining chairs with plastic cane-like seats
on Craig's List for $65 the lot;
the two warped bent-wood Boliden chairs ($99.99 each)
are out on the deck now where they sit crooked and askew;
a homeless person has probably made a shelter of the
two medium sized low pile polypropylene rugs ($99.99 each).

I got the message.
And cut up the Fjellse untreated wood double bed frame ($49.99)
and the Förhöja kitchen cart ($89.99) for firewood.
Being lousy wood, they burned too quickly.

My study is sacrosanct
and so dirty and dusty that my wife rarely goes near it.
But even I know that the rickety Goliat computer desk ($68.99),
with coffee, ink, and alcohol stains, is junk;
its shakiness drives me nuts and cries: firewood! firewood!

But the plain Golant table-top ($80)? It has legs!
It's as comfortable as an old sweater.
It's mine.
You've gotta know when to hold...

The Golden Gate Bridge

The stunning orange-vermillion Bridge spans the entrance to the
beautiful Bay
and looks both north and south
like the two-faced Roman gatekeeper god Janus.
When completed in 1937,
held together by 1,200,000 rivets,
this architectural wonder
was the longest suspension bridge in the world;
its two main cables, 3 feet in diameter,
contain 27,572 strands (80 thousand miles) of wire;
its end-anchoring piers are each composed of
750 million pounds of concrete;
in high winds the Bridge sways 27 feet
and flexes 10 feet;
forty million cars and one million pedestrians
cross the Bridge every year.

The panoramic views from the Bridge,
a shining symbol of California
and its loveliest city, are magical:
the vast undulating Pacific Ocean,
the brownish grassy slopes and ridges
and surf-sprayed rocky coast of the Marin Headlands;
the Tiburon Peninsula,
its fine homes dangling precariously from cliffs;

Alcatraz, Angel Island,
Buena Vista and Treasure islands, the Bay Bridge;
greater San Francisco, lovely in the sun;
the Bay itself, speckled with sailboats and whitecaps
like a field of white wildflowers.
In summer you'll see a line of sailboats
outside the Bridge straining to hold their places
against the strong ebb tide, waiting for the change to flood
so they can re-enter the Bay.

Yet the Bridge's beauty calls to both life and death:
like the Sirens of mythology
the alluring Bridge is a lethal beauty,
a seductive, mystical magnet for jumpers
who smash into the rock-hard water at 80 miles per hour
and shatter and burst.

Just as the sailboats push against the tide,
so the disheartened struggle against depression:
"At every climax, trapped, alone,
You seem to be a helpless passenger that drifts
On some frail boat…
As from a distance,
watch yourself disintegrate in foaming seas."
– Weldon Kees.
The poet, after a last look around,
(his body never found)
jumped from the bewitching Bridge in 1955.
Few who jump survive.

I met Ed Curran for the first time in fifty years and we have
become good friends. We would not have recognized each other. Ed

went to the Naval Academy and is an engineer: he helped build the airport in Riyadh, Saudi Arabia. He is a grizzled guy and tough. He has had open heart surgery and has chronic back pain for some time. Ed lives in San Anselmo, California and we go sailing together. Two incidents are worth mentioning. In the first we were sailing from Sausalito to San Francisco and the swells were very large and the wind was howling hard coming from under the Golden Gate Bridge. We couldn't get turned around and were headed toward the shore. Finally, we got turned around in time and headed back to Sausalito. Another time the weather was okay but, during a jibe, we lost the mast. It was a deck-stepped mast and the point where it connected to the deck was all messed up. We were spotted by the Coast Guard and told to pull into the Hyde Street dock where there was room for guests. When we got there Carolyn had been hit in the head by the mast so we went to a bar and got her an icepack. Ed, in the meantime, was pulling up the mast and wires and cracked two ribs. We finally got all the rigging off, dropped the whole contraption in the water, and motored home.

My second wife, Carolyn Saito, was a Japanese American born in Chicago and raised in the Bay Area. She was nine years younger than I and a good person. We went on a cruise through the Panama Canal. We also went horse-back riding. And we went on an overnight cruise in the ocean from San Francisco to half Moon Bay. We also went to New Zealand where it rained all the time. I remember watching the Keas or Mountain Parrot attacking the rubber tires and windshield wipers of cars. We also went on a cruise in Alaska, in a small boat. There were six passengers and six crew members. It was beautiful country and we came back to Seattle where the boat was wintered. We went whale watching off of Point Reyes and saw many whales very close up. The whales were apparently chasing the krill which were under the boat. We came within five feet of them. Carolyn and I took a train trip from Toronto to Vancouver, intending to go over the Canadian Rockies Mountains, and we got off at Jasper, rented a car and went down to Lake Louise. When we tried to go back to Jasper to the train it was snowing hard and the road was closed. We went a little ways north and I wrote the following:

Snow

"Sure is pretty here. I'm driving slowly because of the snow. It's a little slippery."

"I know."

"At least we're not in a blizzard."

"I know. Still, it's been snowing for three days."

"To be honest I wish we had your SUV instead of this rented car."

"That would be better."

"With the four-wheel drive, I mean."

"I know, Dave."

"Where we turned off the highway, the sign said Johnston Falls 27 kilometers."

"How far is that?"

"About 17 miles, I think."

"It must be beautiful. The guide book said it has metal walkways so you can walk on the ice. Like that frozen falls we saw on the way down from Jasper the other day.

"Yeah. It'll be great. We'll get some good pictures."

"We've been driving for half an hour and haven't seen a single other car on this road."

"You're right."

"There's nothing but forest here. Maybe no else is foolish enough to be on this road in this weather."

"I know how to drive in this stuff, Carolyn. I really do."

"I know you do."

"I'm trying to stay in these old tracks, which must be from

yesterday. I hope the snow in the center of the tracks doesn't get too high. Once in while I hear scraping under the car."

"I know. You sure we shouldn't turn around?"

"The road's too narrow to turn around. Good chance we'd get stuck. Anyway, like I said, I know how to drive in this stuff."

"I know."

"Yeah. I drove a lot in snow in New Hampshire. We came to see Johnston Falls, remember?"

"Okay."

"At least going forward we're moving."

"Why are you so quiet now?"

"No reason, I'm just thinking. It's snowing harder. Turn up the defroster."

"Okay. But I think we should turn around now."

"Maybe you're right."

"Try it. I think we should get out of here."

"Okay. I'll try it. Here we go, slowly...very slowly... Damn, it's too narrow. I don't want to push it. If we get off onto the shoulder we're in trouble."

"Please try something else."

"Remember how the road split around those trees so it was one way each way for a while? If the road splits again I'll try and turn around where it rejoins."

"Okay. I'm getting a little worried."

"Nothing really to worry about. Do you have a will?"

"No. Why?"

"Just wondered. You should make one, you know."

"Doesn't matter. Everything goes to my children."

"I'm not so sure. Without a will it could get screwed up."

"You might be right."

"Remember that movie we saw, ***Into the Wild***, about the guy who starved to death in the wilderness in Alaska in the winter?"

"Yes. Why do you bring **that** up now?"

"This reminds me of it a little bit. I read the book too, by Jon Krakauer. He writes about extreme situations, such as tragedies on Mt. Everest."

"Oh, great."

"Hey. The road just divided. I'll try to turn around and go the other way when it joins again. Shouldn't be too long."

"I hope not."

"Okay. Here we go…. No…No. I don't dare try this. The snow's too high now. Trying to turn around could be a disaster. What now? Uhum. Uhum. Maybe I can just back out the way we came."

"You must be nuts. You can't back up all the way."

"Well, I'm gonna try. Here goes…Oops. Christ, we're slipping sideways. This'll never work."

"I knew that. I'm really kind of scared, Dave. What are we going to do?"

"You're the navigator, sweetie. You remember if this road comes in to another road, or just goes to Johnston Falls?"

"I don't remember."

"If the road dead ends at Johnston Falls were cooked."

"What do you mean cooked?"

"Never mind. If worse comes to worst, we can always use your cell phone."

"My cell phone's in the hotel."

"Ugh. Might not have worked here anyway. Do we have anything to eat?"

"No, just some mints in my purse."

"Any water?"

"Just one small bottle, and it's frozen."

"If we get stuck or run out of gas we'll have to walk out. Or should I walk out for help while you stay here?"

"What about the car?"

"Who cares about the car?"

"I'm not staying here by myself."

"Okay. But it's cold and the snow is getting worse."

"Look. There's a sign. Johnston Falls…I can barely make it out in the snow …8 kilometers I think."

"The hell with Johnston Falls. I wonder if there's wolves around here? Like the one we saw yesterday on the way to Sunshine Valley. I bet there's bears too. Once in Yosemite I saw a car door that was ripped off by a bear."

"Oh, great."

"I once read it takes about three hours for a human to freeze."

"Oh please."

"I don't wanna be here at night. This is getting really hairy."

"Geez."

"Hey look. There's a house or something. On the left."

"I see it. Looks like a store. And there's a little gas pump."

"Oh. Whew. That's good. I'm so glad. There's a parking place and the snow's tamped down. I can see pavement."

"Find out what's going on around here."

"Ah. There. We're stopped. I'm going in. I've got a tension headache and stomach hurts'

"Why were you so long?"

"I really had to pee. I smoked two cigarettes. I'm sweating even though it's cold."

"Where are we?"

"The guy inside said we go left here and the highway is about a quarter mile beyond a little bridge. He said we were paralleling the highway the whole time. That is was always just a few hundred yards away."

"I can't believe it? Anyway, thank heavens. I almost thought…"

"Okay, we're off. Hey, there's route 1 South."

"Thank God!"

"Let's go back to Banff."

"I can use a drink."

"I can use two drinks. And a bottle of aspirin. Then two more drinks."

So we went back to Lake Louise, spent the night and went to Calgary the next day to head back to San Francisco on the plane. I was bitter cold in Calgary and the wind was blowing hard. We found a hotel and standing around outside in the wind were six or seven beautiful women all gussied up for the evening—it turned out they were gay men. The hockey team the San Jose Sharks were playing the Calgary Flames the next day so the Sharks and the gay men all sat down to breakfast together.

Later, my parrot, Streak, died accidentally from fumes from Teflon (which are deadly to birds). So I got another bird, an African Grey. But he flew away when it was on my shoulder while I was getting the mail and was never found. So I got another African Gray, named Blossom, who is a good companion.

I have now become blind in the left eye, completely blind and not restorable. The doctors think it is related to the Vasculitis. I tried to buy another pistol in case I go blind in the other eye. I don't want to live completely blind. But now I am on the California no firearms list.

"Dave I've Had It!"

When he said "Dave I've had it!" I put the phone down
And ambled over to his Marina flat.
It was spring: bird song in trees, blue sky, skirts high.
Through the glass-fronted newspaper box I read
"Alien with five heads and six arms found in well."
Ate a glazed donut, sweet and fresh.
Gave money to the "Rescue the Stray Cats" girl.
Watched boys throw baseballs in the park.
I found Jack drowned in a tubful of bloody water.
I had thought about doing that too.
Who got the best deal?

I went to a movie.
The popcorn was so buttery and good.

I have become an increasingly good squash player since I joined the University Club of San Francisco. I play doubles only and am rated number six or seven in North America in my age bracket. I've always been a racquets man.

What Men Want

I want to stroll down Geary Street near Union Square
in a tailor-made dark blue Cashmere
Cesare Attolini double-vented light-weight suit,
with a yellow Hermes pocket square,
a light blue French-cuffed dress shirt
open two buttons at the neck,
and black Bruno Magli ankle boots of the softest leather.
I want to turn heads:
the women's with a spark of desire,
the men's with a jolt of envy.
I want the store clerks at Macy's,
where I buy monogrammed handkerchiefs,
to notice I don't wear a wedding ring
and to whisper about me.
I want the baker's wife at the Boulangerie Florian
to look up coyly at me as she brings my espresso.
I want the policewoman to put her hand on her pistol butt
when she sees me.
I want the meter-maid
to stop writing that ticket for a moment.
I want the woman window-shopping for a Fendi handbag
to startle and to stare at my reflection.

I want people to know I live in a big house
and to wonder what kind of car I drive.
I want the one in the black <u>Oscar de la Renta</u>
silk sponge crepe dress
to lock eyes with me and hesitate before going
into the Westin- St. Francis hotel to meet her paltry lover.
I want them all to sense my cool self-confidence and dignity
and to be awed by the maleness and mystery of me.
But that woman bursting out
of her cheap sleeveless and backless red dress,
with spiked heels, who's all dusky curves and come on:
I want to rip her clothes off...

If I am anything I am a Buddhist. It is a good religion and psychology. I have read heavily in Buddhism and gone to Plum Village, which is Thich Nath Hahn's (the Zen Buddhist) spiritual community in the Dordogne Valley in France. I went there with both my sons and stayed there for two weeks. I'm also an agnostic and perhaps a pantheist. I find great power and mystery in nature.

My third wife is Julie Duncan, who is 21 years younger than I. She has brown shoulder length hair, blue eyes, and is curvy and petite. She is cool and sweet and has a dog named Tanner, a mix between a Dachshund and a Sheltie. Tanner and my new African Grey parrot keep good company for each other. I have written a children's book about them entitled *Tanner, Blossom and the Evil Weevil*. Time will tell what adventures Julie and I will have, but they'll be god ones. And best of all, I haven't been depressed for several years, which is contrary to the received wisdom that older people, if they are bi-polar or depressives, get increasingly ill.

End

Printed in the United States
By Bookmasters